A Guide to Starting Your Own Profitable Dog Walking Business

Anthony Rio James

Table of Contents

Introduction

Humans and their canine friends share a very unique relationship. Dogs provide unending affection, fidelity, and business. Dogs are treasured family members for many people, not simply pets. A dog may bring enormous joy and unconditional love into one's life in an often chaotic and stressful environment. However, the demands of our hectic schedules frequently prevent us from giving our furry friends the exercise and outside experiences they require to have fulfilling lives.

Here's where the dog walking industry becomes relevant. Walking dogs is more than just a job for me; it's a passion. Its goal is to provide owners peace of mind while assisting dogs in maintaining their happiness, health, and activity levels. It's about making your passion for dogs into a successful business. This book is your guide to making your dream of spending your days outside, surrounded by wagging tails and moist noses, come true if you genuinely love your four-legged pets.

We'll take you on a tour of the fascinating dog-walking world on the following pages. The fundamentals of the dog walking business, how to become ready for business ownership, what kind of training and abilities are necessary, and the day-to-day operations of starting a business will all be covered. We'll explore branding, marketing, cultivating and maintaining client relationships, and business growth tactics. We'll also talk about typical problems and hazards you can encounter and how to prepare for long-term success while acknowledging your accomplishments.

Now, grab a leash and begin your journey to being a prosperous dog walker. From your first dog walk to a successful dog walking business, this comprehensive book is made to help you negotiate every step of the journey—whether you're an ambitious entrepreneur or a pet lover trying to turn your hobby into a career.

Chapter 1: Introduction to the Dog Walking Business

(Figure: 01)

The dog walking sector has flourished in recent years due mainly to the rising demand for pet care services. Pet owners have employed professional dog walkers to provide dogs with the necessary exercise and business when their owners cannot do so because of job obligations, physical restrictions, or other circumstances. Dog walking has grown in popularity as a lucrative job choice for many entrepreneurs and animal lovers as more people realize how important it is to keep their pets active and healthy lifestyles.

The way pet owners' lifestyles are evolving is one of the main factors contributing to the expansion of the dog walking industry. With lengthy work hours and hectic schedules, modern life is frequently fast paced. This makes it difficult for many pet owners to give their pets the time and care they need. Dogs are social creatures, and to keep them physically and emotionally well, they require frequent exercise, mental stimulation, and social connection. Professional dog walkers fill this gap by providing pet owners with a dependable and practical alternative.

The dog walking service serves a diverse clientele. Not only does it serve working adults, but it also serves the elderly, people with disabilities, and those recuperating from diseases or accidents. The dog walking business can function as a vital resource for the entire community because of its diverse clientele, which also helps make it inclusive and accessible. In addition, dog walking services are not just needed in cities; they are also highly sought after in suburban and rural environments, meaning the business may prosper in various situations.

Dog-walking businesses sometimes need little initial capital, which makes them a desirable choice for aspiring people to become self-employed as its also flexible. Typically, the most significant costs are associated with marketing, insurance, and acquiring necessary dog walking gear, including leashes and waste bags. One may build a reliable clientele and generate consistent revenue with the correct business plan and marketing approach. Maintaining and expanding a profitable dog-walking business requires developing a solid reputation and trust in the neighborhood.

The dog walking industry plays a critical role in bridging the gap between the needs of busy pet owners and their four-legged friends. This field promises a bright future for people who are genuinely enthusiastic about animals and are committed to giving them competent and sensitive care. Dog walking is expected to be a significant profession within the larger pet care industry as more people realize how important it is to keep their dogs happy and healthy.

Understanding the Pet Industry

The pet business is a large and continuously growing sector that includes many goods and services to satisfy pet owners' and their animals' requirements and preferences. The pet market is diverse and constantly changing, from grooming services and pet insurance to pet food and medical care. Examining this industry's fundamental elements, current developments, and growth-promoting variables is crucial to thoroughly understanding it.

Elements of the Pet Sector:

1. Pet Food and Nutrition: The manufacturing and distribution of pet food account for a sizeable chunk of the pet sector. This covers a range of diets, from canned and kibbled meals to raw and organic foods. The pet food market emphasizes customized diets that meet specific health requirements.
2. Pet health and veterinary services: The pet business is incomplete without veterinary care. This covers regular physicals, shots, operations, and prescription drugs. There is now a developing market for pet insurance to assist with paying for veterinary treatment.

3. Pet Supplies and Accessories: This section includes collars, leashes, crates, toys, and bedding. Businesses frequently launch stylish and cutting-edge items to satisfy pet owners' needs for their four-legged companions.
4. Pet Grooming and Care: Mobile grooming units, spas, and salons are among the increasingly popular pet grooming services. Pet owners might find a handy option in pet boarding and daycare services, in addition to grooming, while they are away.
5. Pet Technology: With the creation of intelligent pet collars, pet monitoring gadgets, automatic feeds, and even AI-powered pet care robots, the pet tech industry is increasing. These gadgets make it easier for pet owners to watch and communicate with their animals from a distance.

Important Pet Industry Trends:

1. Humanization of Pets: As more people view their animals as part of the family, there is a growing need for specialized and high-quality goods and services.
2. Wellness and Health: More organic, natural, and functional pet food alternatives are available due to the increased emphasis on nutrition and animal health.

Additionally, owners are more likely to seek preventative medical treatment for their animals.

3. E-commerce: Pet owners now have easy access to an extensive range of alternatives and convenience thanks to the rise in online sales of pet items.
4. Sustainability: As pet owners become more aware of how pet goods affect the environment, there is a growing desire for environmentally friendly and sustainable solutions.
5. Pet Services: As busy lives necessitate more help with pet care, services like dog walking, pet sitting, and pet training have grown significantly.

Elements Promoting Growth:

1. Demographics: The need for pet companionship has grown due to an aging population and increased single-person homes.
2. Urbanization: Due to space constraints, people in cities frequently choose smaller pets, which impacts the range of goods and services available.
3. Benefits to Human Health: Several research have demonstrated how having a pet may improve human health, including lowering stress and loneliness. These

findings provide another justification for pet ownership.

4. Social Media and Influencers: The popularity of pets and pet-related material on social media platforms has increased demand for stylish pet items and interest in pet ownership.

The humanization of pets, shifting cultural trends, and the need for high-quality goods and services have all contributed to the growth of the pet business, which is a dynamic and varied sector. Businesses and entrepreneurs hoping to enter or succeed in this lucrative and dynamic sector must understand the industry's constituent parts, trends, and motivating factors. There is still room for innovation and growth in the pet market as owners look for methods to improve the lives of their cherished animals.

The Growing Demand for Dog Walking Services

The need for expert dog walking services has significantly increased in the last several years. Numerous variables, reflecting shifts in pet owners' preferences and lives, are driving this development. Here's a closer look at the factors driving the rising demand for dog walking services:

1. Busy Lifestyles: Long workdays, commuting, and hectic schedules are standard features of modern life. It might be difficult for many pet owners to set aside enough time for their dogs' exercise and social requirements. For these people, dog walking services provide a helpful option that guarantees their pets the required mental and physical stimulation.
2. Urbanization: Dog owners find it more challenging to provide their pets with enough exercise because urban regions tend to have fewer green spaces and smaller housing. The need for dog walkers who can take dogs for walks, playdates, and outdoor experiences in surrounding parks has increased due to this urban lifestyle.
3. Rise in Pet Ownership: Both the quantity and variety of pet owners have been rising over time and especially due to COVID-19 With more individuals adopting pets, there is a natural increase in demand for services like dog walking, which can accommodate a wider variety of breeds and personalities.
4. Pet Health and Well-Being: More and more pet owners understand the value of consistent exercise for their canines' physical and emotional health. Frequent

exercise can improve general quality of life, reduce behavioral issues, and avoid obesity. To maintain the happiness and health of their dogs, many pet owners are prepared to spend money on professional dog walking services.

5. Aging Population: As people age, more pet owners may have physical restrictions that make walking their pets challenging. Dog walking services are an invaluable resource for those unable to care for their dogs due to physical limitations.
6. Pet Humanization: Pets are now viewed as family members, and owners are more likely to give their animals the same love and care they provide to their human family members. This involves engaging seasoned caretakers like dog walkers to accommodate their dogs' requirements.
7. Pet socialization: canines are social creatures, and their mental and emotional health depends on their regular engagement with people and other canines. Group walks are a common feature of dog walking services, allowing canines to mingle and enjoy business.

8. Convenience and Peace of Mind: Dog owners appreciate the ease and tranquility of hiring an expert dog walker. It gives them comfort and peace of mind to know that their dogs are cared for throughout the day by a trustworthy and trained person.

The number of dog walking companies and individual dog walkers has increased in response to the rising demand for dog walking services. These experts frequently provide various services, from quick walks to long adventures, to satisfy the growing demand and ensure that there are alternatives for all dog types and activity levels. Dog walking services are predicted to stay in high demand if pet owners prioritize their animals' happiness and well-being, making them a viable and long-term business opportunity in the pet care sector.

The Benefits of Starting a Dog Walking Business

Establishing a dog walking business may be fulfilling and successful with several advantages. The following are some benefits of starting and maintaining a dog-walking business:

1. Passion and Love for Dogs: If you have an affinity for animals, owning a dog walking business will give you

daily opportunities to interact with canines. Spending time with these devoted and affectionate creatures may be rewarding and delightful.

2. Flexibility: Regarding scheduling, dog walking companies frequently provide much flexibility. Walking dogs gives you flexibility in terms of when and where you walk them, which makes juggling work and other obligations or personal commitments simpler.
3. Inexpensive Initial Costs: A dog walking business has very affordable initial costs compared to many other business ventures. Leashes, trash bags, and maybe marketing materials are the only necessities; otherwise, your overhead expenses won't be as expensive as for many other enterprises.
4. High Demand: As busy pet owners look for dependable and trustworthy specialists to ensure their pets get the exercise and socializing, they require, the demand for dog walking services is steadily rising. There is a constant flow of prospective customers due to this persistent need.
5. Scalability: You may hire more dog walkers or broaden your service area as your business expands

and you acquire expertise, increasing your potential revenue.

6. Community Involvement: Owning a dog walking business enables you to integrate deeply into your neighborhood. You may improve your community's pet welfare while fostering ties with nearby pet owners.
7. Healthy Lifestyle: Walking dogs for a living gets you outside and moving. It's physically demanding work that may improve your fitness and general health. Additionally, spending time with dogs might help you feel less stressed and more mentally healthy.
8. Personal Fulfillment: Many dog owners value your vital service by ensuring their animals receive the exercise and attention they require. As you improve the lives of dogs and their owners, this may be personally satisfying.
9. Repeat Business: Offering dog walking services might result in returning customers. You may establish enduring connections and a steady clientele, guaranteeing a consistent cash flow because dog owners need continuing care for their pets.

10. Opportunity for Diversification: Although walking dogs is your primary service, you may expand your business's income potential by providing other pet-related services like pet sitting, lodging, or even pet transportation.
11. Low Risk: There aren't many dangers involved in running a dog walking business if proper planning and management are practiced. Having the right insurance may protect you and your clients in unforeseen circumstances.
12. Opportunities for Specialization: You can focus on particular tasks, such as dealing with elderly dogs, pets with special requirements, or dogs of a specific breed. You may be able to charge more for your skills if you specialize.

Establishing and maintaining a dog walking business involves commitment, conscientious pet care, and top-notch customer support. Building confidence with your clients is crucial, as is putting the security and welfare of the pets under your supervision first. A dog walking business may be gratifying and financially rewarding if you truly love dogs and are prepared to do the work.

Setting Realistic Goals and Expectations

Achieving both personal and professional success requires setting reasonable expectations and goals. Setting goals for your personal, professional, or any other area of your life may help you stay motivated and focused if you know what is unrealistic. Here's how to manage reasonable expectations and goals:

1. Identify Your Goals: Begin by outlining your objectives. What goals do you have in mind? Establish clear, exact goals when you set them. For instance, state, "I want to earn a promotion within the next 12 months," rather than, "I want to be more successful at work."
2. Create SMART goals: SMART is specific, measurable, achievable, relevant and time bound. Be sure your objectives fit these requirements. Particular objectives are precise and well-defined. Quantifiable objectives have success criteria that can be measured. Realistic and reachable objectives are attainable. Relevant goals complement your long-term goals and values. Time-bound objectives have a due date.
3. Recognize Your Limitations: Assess your advantages and disadvantages. Consider your time limits, abilities,

and resources. A goal you set for yourself that involves resources or skills you don't have might make you unhappy.

4. Break Down Bigger Goals: If your main objective is essential, divide it into smaller, easier-to-achieve sub-objectives. This lessens the sense of overload on the journey and facilitates efficient tracking of your advancement.
5. Prioritize Your Objectives: Ascertain which objectives are most crucial and pertinent to your life. Setting your priorities can help you concentrate on the things that count.
6. Research and Learn: Do your homework and obtain knowledge to determine what is practically achievable before establishing any expectations or goals. This will assist you in setting objectives that are grounded in reality rather than fantasy.
7. Have Patience: Recognize that it will take time to accomplish your goals. Rome wasn't built in a day, and significant achievements usually needed persistence and dedication.
8. Modify Your Objectives: Remain flexible in modifying your objectives when situations evolve. Since life is

ever-changing, what seems reasonable now could not be so tomorrow. Being adaptable is essential for long-term success.

9. Seek Support and Feedback: Talk to mentors, family members, or trustworthy friends about your expectations and aspirations. They may offer insightful advice and assist you in establishing reasonable expectations.
10. Control Yourself-Criticism: Be kind and try not to be too hard on yourself. Acknowledge that obstacles and disappointments are a part of the process and can offer insightful lessons.
11. Appreciate Little Wins: Acknowledge and appreciate your accomplishments no matter how modest they appear. Acknowledging your progress helps you stay motivated and inspires you to work more.
12. Remain Committed: Achieving goals needs perseverance and commitment. Remember your long-term goals and be dedicated to achieving them.

You may prevent dissatisfaction and fatigue by establishing reasonable expectations and goals. While pushing oneself is vital, being realistic and patient in your quest for achievement is critical. You'll have a better chance of accomplishing your objectives and staying happy when you take this well-rounded strategy.

Legal and Regulatory Considerations

A vital component of running any organization is considering legal and regulatory factors. Violating relevant rules and regulations may result in severe legal and financial ramifications. When launching and operating a firm, keep the following important legal and regulatory factors in mind:

1. Business Structure: Select the appropriate legal framework for your business. A corporation, limited liability business (LLC), partnership, sole proprietorship, and other forms of organization are common choices. There are various legal and tax ramifications for each arrangement.
2. Registered Business: Depending on the nature of your business, you might have to register it with the relevant government agencies, such as the state or county, and get the required licenses and permissions.
3. Taxes: Recognize your federal, state, and municipal tax responsibilities. This covers employment taxes, sales taxes, income taxes, and any other applicable taxes.

Maintain correct financial documentation to guarantee adherence.

4. Employment Laws: If you have workers, you should be knowledgeable about state and federal employment laws, which cover things like workers' compensation obligations, workplace safety standards, anti-discrimination legislation, and wage and hour restrictions.
5. Intellectual Property: If relevant, safeguard your intellectual property, including patents, copyrights, and trademarks. Ensure that neither your business name nor your merchandise violates anybody else's intellectual property rights.
6. Contracts: When making agreements, be explicit and exact. When creating or revising a contract, seek legal advice to safeguard your interests and ensure all conditions are enforceable.
7. Privacy and Data Protection: You might have to abide by data protection and privacy regulations if you gather, maintain, or process personal information about clients or staff members. Each jurisdiction may have quite different rules.

8. Environmental restrictions: You might have to abide by environmental limits, such as those about energy efficiency, waste management, and emissions standards, depending on your sector.
9. Zoning and Land Use: Verify that the location of your firm conforms with land use and zoning laws. Certain enterprises can need unique zoning approvals.
10. Health and Safety Regulations: You must abide by specific rules and license requirements if your business deals with food preparation, childcare, healthcare, or other sectors that impact public health and safety.
11. Online Business Regulations: You might have to abide by specific rules about digital privacy, online sales tax, and online consumer protection if your business runs an online store or engages in e-commerce.
12. Financial Reporting: Transparency and accuracy in financial reporting are essential. Recognize accounting standards, including generally accepted accounting principles (GAAP) and any reporting requirements for your industry.

13. Employee Benefits: Ensure you know your legal responsibilities if you provide your staff retirement plans or health insurance.
14. Insurance: To safeguard your business from unanticipated occurrences like liability claims, property damage, or natural catastrophes, you must have enough insurance coverage.
15. Regulatory Changes: Over time, laws and regulations may be modified. Keep abreast of legal developments that affect your sector or area and be ready to alter your business procedures, as necessary.
16. Consumer Protection: Adhere to rules about fair business practices, product safety, and advertising to safeguard consumers.

Speaking with legal and financial experts specializing in business concerns is essential to guarantee complete compliance with these legal and regulatory requirements. To further show your dedication to compliance and shield your business from legal problems, maintain total records and paperwork for your business operations.

Chapter 2: Preparing for Your Dog Walking Business

(Figure: 02)

Careful planning and preparation are necessary when starting a dog walking business to guarantee both the profitability of the venture and the welfare of the dogs you will be managing. The following are crucial actions to think about when getting ready to launch your dog-walking business:

1. Research and Market Analysis: Start with a local market analysis to determine the need for dog walking services. Determine who your target market is—busy professionals, senior pet owners, etc.—and evaluate the competition in your field. You will be able to assess your business's potential with the aid of this research.
2. Business Strategy: Make a thorough business plan that outlines your business's objectives, goals, and financial predictions. A well-organized strategy can act as a growth roadmap for your business and may be an effective means of attracting investors or funding.
3. Legal Aspects: Decide on your business's legal form, such as an LLC or sole proprietorship, then register it with the relevant authorities. Acquire any required licenses or permissions and ensure that local laws are followed.
4. Insurance: To safeguard your business if any mishaps or injuries involving the dogs in your care occur, get insurance coverage, such as liability insurance. Talk to an insurance professional about your needs to obtain the proper coverage.

5. Certification and Training: Acquiring the information and abilities required to care for dogs safely is crucial. Consider enrolling in dog behavior and pet first aid classes and perhaps earning a certification in dog training. Obtaining certificates might help you get more trust from clients.
6. Equipment and goods: Get the goods and equipment your dog walking business will require. This includes leashes, waste bags, water bowls, and other equipment needed to handle and care for dogs.
7. Cost and Amenities: Determine the variety of services you will provide and your pricing strategy. To reach a wider clientele, consider the competitive pricing in your region and consider providing different packages or add-on services, such as pet sitting or pet transportation.
8. Safety Protocols: To protect the welfare of the dogs you walk, create, and follow safety protocols. This entails handling possible hazards during walks, appropriately restraining dogs, and comprehending dog behavior.
9. Customer Agreements: Draft thorough, unambiguous client contracts that specify your offerings, payment

terms, cancelation guidelines, and restrictions on your liability. These agreements safeguard your consumers as well as you.

10. Marketing and Branding: To advertise your dog walking service, create a compelling brand identity and marketing plan. A business website, social media presence, and online or print ads in pet-related magazines or periodicals in the area are a few examples of this.
11. Record-keeping: To help you schedule appointments, monitor client information, and retain vital health records for the dogs under your care, set up a system for scheduling and record-keeping.
12. Client Screening: Establish a procedure for vetting prospective clients and their canines. This guarantees a fantastic fit and assists in identifying any unique requirements, inclinations, or habits you should be mindful of.
13. Emergency Preparedness: Make sure you're ready for anything unexpected by planning for mishaps, injuries, and lost dogs. Keep a first aid kit and be prepared to handle frequent pet emergencies.

14. Client Communication: Continue to communicate with your clients honestly and efficiently. After every walk, provide updates, answer questions immediately, and professionally handle any issues or requests.

You'll be better positioned to offer your clients high-quality services and earn their confidence if you follow these preparation measures before starting your dog walking business. It is essential to remember that the safety and well-being of the pets in your care should come first. Additionally, keeping up a high standard of professionalism will make you stand out in a crowded market.

Market Research and Identifying Your Niche

Finding a niche and conducting thorough market research are essential to creating a profitable business. Knowing your market and finding your specialization helps put you on the right track when launching or growing a business, especially one that involves walking dogs. This is the method to follow:

Market Analysis:

1. Establish Your Goals: Set clear objectives for your study first. What particular details are you looking for?

Do you want to evaluate the competition, determine market trends, or choose the demand in your region for dog walking services?

2. Analyze the Population: Examine your target market's demographics. Consider variables like geography, household size, age, and income. You may better customize your services for potential customers with this information.
3. Evaluate the Competition: List and evaluate your dog walking industry rivals. Ascertain the number of dog walkers or pet care providers in your neighborhood, then assess their reputation, offerings, and costs.
4. Collect Data: To gather data, employ a range of research techniques. Surveys, interviews, internet research, and report analysis from the sector are a few examples of this. Information regarding trends and demand may be found with tools like Google Trends and social media analytics.
5. Assess Market Size: Compute the approximate size of your market. In your location, how many prospective customers are there? Examine variables such as the percentage of people who own pets, the population's

size, and the pet owners' willingness to pay for dog walking services.

6. Recognize Client Needs: Determine the requirements and inclinations of your intended clientele. This may involve elements like the breed of dogs they own, their daily routines, and the particular services they need.

Finding Your Specialization:

1. Examine Your Interests and Skills: Evaluate your abilities, passions, and interests. What are your areas of expertise and enjoyment in the dog walking business? Developing self-awareness might aid in identifying your specialization.
2. Examine the Gaps in the Market: Determine gaps or underserved niches in the dog walking industry based on your market analysis. Specialized services like senior dog care, puppy socialization, or breeds with particular needs, for instance, could be in demand.
3. Assess Customer Needs: discover what prospective customers want but can't find in the already offered dog walking services. After hearing what they say, consider how you might meet their unmet needs.
4. Geographic specialty: You may also have a geographic thing. You can decide to concentrate on a particular

town or area where dog owners are more prevalent or where dog walking services are scarcer.

5. Specializations: Consider providing specialty services like dog walking that is environmentally friendly, pet first aid, or training. These might help you stand out in a crowded market.
6. Pricing Strategy: Depending on how you set your prices, you may identify your specialty. You may provide reasonable solutions for pet owners on a tight budget or high-end services for discriminating customers.
7. Marketing Message: Your branding and marketing message might help to convey your specialization. What makes your dog walking service special should be made crystal clear in your unique selling proposition (USP).
8. Networking and Partnerships: Connect with other companies that cater to pets, such as grooming services, pet shops, and vets. Referrals and partnerships might assist you in finding your specialty.
9. Test and Adapt: Evaluate your tactics and offerings as you determine your specialty. Be ready to modify and

improve your strategy in response to criticism and outcomes.

You may set up your dog walking business for success by conducting in-depth market research and choosing a specialization that complements your qualifications and your target business's demands. A clearly defined niche enables you to stand out in a crowded market and serve a particular clientele that values the exceptional services you provide.

Developing a Business Plan

Any firm that wants to succeed must have a well-structured business plan since it acts as a road map for expansion and, if capital is required, helps get investment. The following is a step-by-step strategy for creating an extensive business plan:

1. Executive Summary: This section should start with an executive summary that lists the main ideas in your business plan, such as your mission statement, vision, and a synopsis of your financial predictions. This part needs to give a broad overview of your whole strategy.
2. Business Description: Provide a thorough explanation of your business. Describe your dog walking business's nature, target market, the issue it seeks to

solve, and its unique selling proposition (USP). Talk about the market and industry developments that support the viability of your business.

3. Market Research: Share the results of your market research, together with information on consumer behavior, the pet industry, and local market demographics. Examine your competitors and determine your market niche.
4. Organizational Structure: Specify how your business is organized. Indicate the legal setup (sole proprietorship, LLC, etc.), the responsibilities of the leading players, and their credentials. Tell us about your hiring strategies as your business expands.
5. Products and Services: Describe the services you provide for walking dogs. Provide information about costs, any extra services (such as training or pet sitting), and how your benefits will be delivered. Describe how your offerings cater to the demands and tastes of your clients.
6. Marketing and Sales Strategy: Give a summary of your strategy for marketing and sales. Describe your target demographic, brand identity, and marketing channels (such as local advertising and social media). Discuss

your sales techniques, pricing strategy, and client acquisition and retention plans.

7. Funding Requirements: Describe the required amount of funds and your intended usage if you want funding. Give a summary of the initial expenses, the amount of working capital needed, and the projected demand for funding.
8. Financial estimates: Produce comprehensive economic predictions that include balance sheets, cash flow estimates, and income statements. Provide best-case, worst-case, and most-situations while exercising caution in your estimations.
9. Operations Plan: Describe how your business runs daily. Talk about your workflow, the tools and supplies you'll require, and the measures to guarantee the security and welfare of the dogs under your care.
10. Risk assessment: Identify any dangers and difficulties your business could encounter and provide plans to alleviate or manage them. Consider matters like responsibility, competition in the market, and evolving consumer tastes.
11. Timelines and Milestones: Establish clear deadlines and milestones for your business. This will enable you

to monitor your development and make any required corrections.

12. Departure Strategy: Describe your departure strategy in detail if you want to leave the business. This can entail going public, selling the business, or transferring ownership to a family member.
13. Appendix: Provide supporting documentation, such as the key team members' résumé, market research findings, court records, and extra financial information.
14. Review and Edit: Once your business plan are finished, go over it again to make sure it is structured, clear, and concise. Consider asking mentors, advisers, or experts in your field for their opinions.

Once finished, your business plan is an invaluable resource for funding and growth management for your business. Maintain its current and utilize it as a benchmark to assess your development and adjust to shifts in the industry and your working environment.

Creating a Budget and Financial Projections

A business plan must include financial predictions and a budget. They offer a road map for managing your money and ensuring your dog-walking business is sustainable and financially sound. Here's how to make financial estimates and a budget step-by-step:

1. To begin, make a sales forecast: Start by projecting your income for the coming month or year. Your sales projection must be grounded on reasonable expectations, considering price, marketing initiatives, and market demand. If you provide various services, break this down by service type.
2. Calculate Your Outlay: Make a list of all of your fixed and variable business expenditures. Rent, insurance, and utilities are examples of fixed expenses. Marketing costs, supplies, and pet care equipment are variable expenses.
3. Project your cash flow: Create a cash flow projection to monitor your business's inflow and outflow of funds. The timing of cash flows, costs, and revenue should all be considered in this estimate. It aids in making plans for times when you have more or less.
4. Create a profit and loss or income statement: The income statement, usually published monthly or yearly, displays your business's profitability over time. To determine your net profit or loss, it shows your revenue and subtracts your costs.

5. Create a sheet of balances: The balance sheet gives you a quick overview of your business's financial situation at a particular moment. It enumerates your proprietor's equity, liabilities, and assets. Liabilities might be loans or unpaid bills, whereas assets can include cash, machinery, and accounts receivable.
6. Take Break-Even Analysis into Account: Determine your break-even point or the end at which your total revenue and costs equal one another, and you have no profit or loss. Knowing your break-even point enables you to make well-informed decisions and create financial goals.
7. Employ Tools or Software for Financial Projection: Consider utilizing internet templates or financial forecast tools to make things easier. You may build and maintain your budget and predictions using tools like Google Sheets, Excel, or professional accounting software.
8. Maintain Realism and Conservatism: Use cautious approximations while constructing your financial predictions. Financial difficulties may arise from either overestimating earnings or underestimating

costs. Consider creating best-case, worst-case, and most-likely scenarios to account for volatility.

9. Take Seasonal Variations into Account: Make sure your financial estimates include any seasonal fluctuations in demand that your dog walking business may encounter. Set up money during busy times to pay for bills during off-peak times.
10. Regularly review and revise: Updating your financial estimates and budget is essential. Please review and update them often to consider modifications to your business, the market, or outside circumstances. This adaptability will enable you to adjust to changing conditions.
11. Look for Expert Advice: Speak with an accountant or financial adviser for advice and experience if you have questions regarding economic predictions or are dealing with significant economic issues for your business.
12. Track and Evaluate Development: Keep a close eye on how your financial performance compares to your estimates. Determine any areas where your budgets or plans may need to be adjusted to achieve your financial objectives.

Creating a budget and economic predictions is a continuing process that can help you make well-informed decisions, get funding, and maintain the financial stability of your dog-walking business. Utilize your budget as a tool to steer your business's economic success, evaluate your financial performance regularly, and adjust to changing conditions.

Naming and Branding Your Business

Creating a memorable name and brand for your dog walking business is essential to building a loyal customer base. The following stages will assist you in selecting the ideal character and creating a powerful brand:

Naming Your Business:

1. Reflect Your Services: Choose a name that accurately describes your business type. A word such as "Paws in Motion Dog Walking" makes it straightforward to prospective customers what your business performs.
2. Distinctive and unforgettable: Pick a name that makes you stand out from the crowd and is distinct and unique. Steer clear of words that are overused, or that might be mistaken for already-existing companies.
3. Consider Your Niche: If you have a particular specialty or niche, include it in your business's name. For

instance, if you are an expert in caring for older dogs, utilize "Golden Paws Senior Dog Walkers."

4. Trademark Check: Verify that the name you have picked for your business is not already a trademark of another business. You can speak with an attorney or search the U.S. Patent and Trademark Office website if needed.
5. Domain Availability: Verify the domain name's availability for your business's website. Online branding and marketing benefit significantly from having a corresponding domain name.
6. Verify that the name you wish to use is accessible for business registration in your community by checking for local business registration. To function lawfully, you must register your business name in several areas.
7. Evaluate the Name: To find out how friends, relatives, or prospective customers feel about the name, ask them for their opinions. Does it make sense to them and strike a chord with them?

Developing a Business Brand:

1. Design a Logo: Make a polished logo that accurately captures the essence of your business. A simple, memorable logo that captures the spirit of your

services is what you want. You could wish to include dog-related details in the layout.

2. Color Scheme: Select a palette of colors to use in your branding. Think of hues that inspire confidence and dependability, such as green and blue, frequently connected to the outdoors and animals.
3. Tagline: Create a catchy slogan that encapsulates your business's goal or distinctive selling proposition and goes well with your name. Think about the song "Where Every Walk Is a Tail-Wagging Adventure."
4. Professional Website: Invest in a website that presents your offerings, costs, and client endorsements. Make sure the website is responsive to mobile devices and easy to use.
5. Social Media Presence: Make an online presence on sites like Facebook and Instagram. Post interesting information about fun activities, safety precautions, and dog care to increase your business's online visibility.
6. Consistent Branding: Make sure your logo is the same on all your marketing collateral, including flyers, social media profiles, and business cards. Brand recognition is increased by consistency.

7. Customer Testimonials: Include gratifying customer reviews on your website and other materials. Testimonials establish credibility and confidence.
8. Expert Photography: Display your dog walking experiences with well-taken, masterful images on your website and promotional materials. These images need to highlight the dogs you've walked and your services ideally.
9. Customer Service: Provide outstanding customer support. A significant element of your brand is how you handle your customers' pets. Positive client interactions encourage word-of-mouth recommendations.
10. Promote your business through local advertising, networking with other pet-related companies, and participating in pet expos and community activities.

Remember that your business name and branding will shape many potential customers' initial impressions of your dog walking service. Make sure it stands out in a crowded market by conveying your expertise, dependability, and love of dogs.

Choosing the Right Business Structure

Choosing the proper business structure is crucial when starting your dog-walking business. Your desired design will impact your business's legal, financial, and operational aspects. Here are some common business structures and factors to consider when making your choice:

1. Sole Proprietorship:

- *Ownership:* You are the sole owner of the business.
- *Liability:* You have personal liability for business debts and legal issues.
- *Taxation:* Your business income is reported on your tax return.
- *Simplicity:* Easy to set up and operate with minimal paperwork.
- *Control:* You have complete control over the business.

2. Limited Liability Business (LLC):

- *Ownership:* Can have one or multiple owners (members).
- *Liability:* Provides personal liability protection, separating personal and business assets.
- *Taxation:* Income can be passed through to members' tax returns or taxed as a corporation.

- *Flexibility:* Offers flexibility in management and operating agreements.
- *Credibility:* Can enhance credibility with clients and partners.

3. Partnership:

- *Ownership:* Shared ownership between two or more partners.
- *Liability:* Personal liability for debts and legal matters, similar to a sole proprietorship.
- *Taxation:* Pass-through taxation, with business income reported on partners' returns.
- *Management:* Partners share management responsibilities and decisions.
- *Partnership Agreement:* A legal partnership agreement is recommended to outline roles, responsibilities, and profit-sharing.

4. Corporation (C-Corporation or S-Corporation):

- *Ownership:* Multiple shareholders, with a board of directors managing the business.
- *Liability:* Shareholders have limited liability, with personal assets protected.

- *Taxation:* C-Corporations have double taxation (at the corporate and individual levels), while S-Corporations offer pass-through taxation.
- *Complexity:* More complex to set up and manage, with more stringent compliance requirements.
- *Investor Appeal:* Attractive to investors and potential for stock offerings.

5. Nonprofit Organization:

- *Purpose:* If your dog walking business has a charitable or community-oriented mission, you might consider a nonprofit structure.
- *Tax Benefits:* Eligible for tax-exempt status and can receive tax-deductible donations.
- *Compliance:* Must adhere to strict regulations and report on activities and finances to maintain nonprofit status.

Factors to Consider:

- Liability: Consider the level of personal liability protection you need. Sole proprietors and partnerships have personal liability for business debts and legal issues, while LLCs and corporations offer limited liability.

- Taxation: Think about your preferred tax structure. For example, an LLC can be taxed as a sole proprietorship, partnership, or corporation. Consult a tax advisor to determine the best option for your specific circumstances.
- Ownership: Determine if you'll have partners or shareholders. Sole proprietorships and single-member LLCs have single licenses, while partnerships, multi-member LLCs, and corporations can have multiple owners.
- Compliance and Regulation: Understand your chosen business structure's legal and regulatory requirements. Corporations typically have more compliance obligations than other structures.
- Operational Flexibility: Consider how you want to manage and run your business. Some structures offer more flexibility in management, while others have defined roles and responsibilities.
- Investor or Donor Considerations: Certain structures like corporations or nonprofits may appeal more to investors or donors if you seek external funding or donations.

- Future Growth: Think about your long-term goals. If you anticipate significant growth or changes in ownership, some structures may be more suitable than others.

It's crucial to consult with legal and financial professionals or business advisors when selecting the proper business structure for your dog walking business. Your choice will have long-term implications, so take the time to evaluate your business's specific needs and consider your financial and legal circumstances.

Chapter 3: Essential Skills and Training

(Figure: 03)

To guarantee the security and welfare of the dogs in your care and to establish credibility with customers, operating a successful dog-walking business involves more than simply a passion for animals.

1. A dog walker's thorough grasp of dog behavior is one of the most critical abilities. Understanding the social dynamics of a canine group and reading body language are all essential skills. You should also be able to see indicators of stress or hostility in dogs. In this sense, specialized dog behavior training may be quite helpful.
2. Pet First Aid and CPR: Training in pet first aid and CPR is crucial since accidents and medical crises might occur. Your ability to handle wounds, choking, and other medical emergencies can significantly impact the welfare of the dogs you look for.
3. Fundamental Training Methods: Even if you're not a certified dog trainer, knowing the training fundamentals will help you control the dogs when you take them on walks. This covers abilities including basic obedience, recalling orders, and leash training.
4. Managing Many Dogs: You must manage several dogs safely and efficiently to walk them all at once. This entails keeping an appropriate leash, exercising control, and averting confrontations or excessive enthusiasm.

5. Physical Fitness: You should be physically healthy because walking dogs may be highly taxing. You'll be walking, bending, and doing other physical tasks with dogs for lengthy periods, so endurance and strength are crucial.
6. Time Management: Time management techniques must be effective. Schedules must be followed, dog exercise time must be given, and dogs must be returned to their owners on time. Establishing credibility with consumers requires being dependable and on time.
7. Communication Skills: Effective communication is essential when interacting with dogs and their owners. You must be able to properly and professionally communicate instructions, provide updates on the behavior and health of the dog, and oversee any customer concerns.
8. Understanding Local Rules: Become acquainted with the rules governing dog walks, leash legislation, and license requirements in your community. Adherence to these standards is crucial to prevent legal complications.

9. Customer service: Having excellent customer service abilities is crucial. Dealing with pet owners who entrust you with their cherished pets' care will be your experience. The work involves establishing a good connection, responding to client problems, and providing exceptional service.
10. Business administration: Scheduling, record-keeping, marketing, and financial administration are just a few business facets of operating a dog-walking business. Understanding these components is essential to your business's development and success.

Consider signing up for classes or workshops on dog behavior, pet first aid, and dog training to get these abilities and information. To prove to clients that you are an expert in these fields, get certification. Furthermore, practical experience—obtained through internships with seasoned dog walkers or volunteer work at animal shelters—can offer priceless training and insights into the field. Maintaining the success of your dog walking business while giving the finest care possible to the dogs under your care requires constant learning and dedication to professional development.

Gaining Knowledge About Dog Behavior and Health

It is essential to have a solid grasp of canine behavior and health to operate a profitable dog-walking business and guarantee the welfare of the dogs under your care. To get this expertise, follow these crucial steps:

1. Research Dog Behavior: Invest in official dog behavior education and training courses. Look for canine behavior and psychology classes, workshops, or certifications. Resources and certification programs are provided by associations such as the Association of Professional Dog Trainers (APDT) and the International Association of Canine Professionals (IACP).
2. Examine Books and Publications: Read reliable books and articles about dogs' psychology, training, and behavior. Writers with a wealth of experience in these areas include Ian Dunbar, Karen Pryor, and Patricia McConnell. Keep up on the most recent findings and developments in dog behavior.
3. Attend Workshops and Seminars: Participate in workshops and seminars led by knowledgeable behaviorists and dog trainers. These gatherings offer

practical experience, networking opportunities, and insights into the day-to-day operations of collaborating with dogs.

4. Volunteer or Intern: You might want to consider volunteering at a nearby animal shelter or rescue group. This allows you to socialize with dogs and see how they behave in different settings. Additionally, you may look for internships with reputable behaviorists or dog trainers.
5. Online Resources: You may get a lot of information on the behavior and health of dogs by using online resources such as websites, forums, and webinars. Suitable materials and resources may be found on websites such as the American Kennel Club (AKC) and the American Veterinary Medical Association (AVMA).
6. Join Professional Groups: Join groups that deal with the behavior and health of dogs on a professional level. These groups frequently provide access to recent studies, networking opportunities, and instructional materials.
7. Canine First Aid and Health: Get instruction in canine health and first aid. Taking pet first aid and CPR courses and earning certificates are essential for

managing crises and guaranteeing the security of the canines under your supervision.

8. Consult Veterinarians: Build rapport with veterinary professionals in your area. Having routine checkups with a veterinarian will help you stay informed about immunizations, joint diseases, and preventative treatment and provide insights into dog health.
9. Behavioral Assessment: Gain the capacity to evaluate the temperament and behavior of a dog. Recognize how to assess their hostility, worries, anxiety, and socialization. This evaluation is essential to ensure that dog walks are pleasurable and safe.
10. Ongoing Education: Maintain your dedication to lifelong learning and career advancement. Keeping up with the latest canine behavior and health developments is crucial since it is a constantly changing sector.

If you learn about canine behavior and health, you'll be well-prepared to give the dogs in your care a safe and happy experience. This knowledge will aid your dog walking business, foster client trust, and enable you to provide their cherished dogs with the finest care possible.

First Aid and Emergency Preparedness for Dogs

Being ready for any situation and being able to give first aid to the dogs in your care are vital while operating a dog walking business. To be sure you can react appropriately in an emergency, follow these crucial steps:

1. Pet First Aid Training: Sign up for dog-specific pet first aid and CPR training. These classes include joint diseases, how to manage injuries, and how to save lives with CPR. Programs for accredited training are provided by organizations such as PDSA, PetTech and the PAWAID.
2. First Aid pack: Assemble a comprehensive package designed just for canines. Add necessary supplies, including bandages, gauze, adhesive tape, tweezers, scissors, antiseptic wipes, a digital thermometer, and a muzzle. When going on dog walks, make sure your gear is readily available.
3. Emergency Contacts: Keep track of the phone numbers of nearby vets, animal clinics open around the clock, and the owner of each dog's contact details. It's essential to have quick access to these numbers in an emergency.

4. Recognize frequent canine illnesses: Become acquainted with the symptoms, warning signs, and frequent canine diseases. Recognize the differences between a dog's typical and aberrant behavior.
5. Knowledge of Poison Control: Recognize common home poisons that can harm dogs and know what to do if a dog consumes a poisonous substance. An invaluable resource is the ASPCA Poison Control Center (888-426-4435).
6. Managing Injuries: Acquire the knowledge to manage several types of injuries, including bites, burns, fractures, and cuts. Recognize how to stabilize a hurt dog to be transported safely.
7. Choking Reaction: Be ready to do the Heimlich technique to a choking dog. When a dog is choking on anything, this ability can save its life.
8. Heat and Cold Stress: Recognize the symptoms of hypothermia and heatstroke in dogs. When taking your dog on a walk, be aware of how to prevent certain diseases and give quick care.
9. Transportation Safety: If necessary, plan to take hurt pets to a vet facility. Make sure your car is equipped and safe to carry pets.

10. Instruction and Practice: Review and hone your first aid techniques regularly. Role-playing situations and staying current on events via further education can be part of this.
11. Remain Calm and Communicate: Remaining composed is essential in emergency circumstances. Clear communication should be maintained with the dog's owner and, if required, emergency veterinarian specialists.
12. Client Consent: Talk to dog owners about emergency protocols and get their permission before overseeing any situations involving their animals.
13. Insurance and Liability: Ensure your dog walking business is adequately insured, including liability insurance. This will shield you in the event of mishaps or crises.
14. Local Rules: Educate yourself on the laws in your area about disaster preparedness and pet care. To stay out of legal trouble, compliance with such restrictions is crucial.
15. Document events: Keep thorough records of all events and crises, including the date, time, incident

description, care given, and any measures done in response.

Your ability to administer first aid and your readiness for emergencies may significantly impact the welfare of the dogs in your care. Additionally, it gives your clients confidence since they know their dogs are in good hands.

Effective Dog Handling Techniques

Effective dog handling methods must be used when working as a dog walker to protect the security and welfare of the dogs in your care. Additionally, you may develop trust with the canines and their owners by using these tactics. The following are some essential techniques for managing dogs well:

1. Be Kind and Calm: Be calm and non-threatening while approaching dogs. Steer clear of abrupt movements or loud noises that might frighten them. Allow dogs to come to you at their leisure.
2. Leash Training: Make sure you know how to handle a leash properly. Use a strong leash and keep your pet under control by not tugging or pulling on it. To teach dogs to walk peacefully on a leash, use positive reinforcement.

3. Recognize Body Language: Observe a dog's body language. Recognize aggressive, fearful, or stressed-out behaviors in your pet, such as tucked tails, raised hackles, and growling. Adapt your strategy to the dog's cues.
4. Positive Reinforcement: To reward excellent conduct, apply positive reinforcement strategies. Affection, praise, and treats reinforce good behavior and promote compliance.
5. Consistency: Consistently give directions and expectations. Since dogs like consistency and regularity, it's helpful to use the same cues and signals to help them understand what's expected.
6. Socialization: Make sure the dogs you walk are compatible and well-socialized if you have more than one. Steer clear of circumstances that might spark arguments. Watch how the group interacts and take appropriate action if needed.
7. Safety Equipment: Always carry safety gear, including a dog whistle, an additional leash, or a safe harness. These instruments can support control in a variety of circumstances.

8. Patience: When dealing with dogs, use patience. Some can be hesitant or take their time getting to know you. Give the dog plenty of time to get used to being around you.
9. Make Use of Verbal signals: Establish precise and dependable verbal cues for instructions. When taught and utilized regularly, voice instructions are well-received by dogs.
10. Refrain from Aggression: Never resort to physical force or hostile techniques when working with dogs. Fear and hostility might result from beating, yelling, or giving severe reprimand.
11. Pre-Walk Evaluations: Determine the dog's energy level and mood before walking. Adapt the stroll to the requirements of the dog. An elderly dog could benefit from a slower exercise rate, but an energetic dog might need more.
12. Be Aware of Your surroundings: Take note of your surroundings during walks. Look for dog dangers like traffic, hostile canines, or potentially harmful objects.
13. Communication with Owners: Continue to communicate with dog owners openly and efficiently.

Talk about any worries, behavioral problems, or particular guidelines about each dog.

14. Establish Trust: Trust is vital. A profitable dog-walking business is built on developing trust with the dogs and their owners. Trust is facilitated by dependability, consistency, and a compassionate disposition.
15. Keep Learning: Stay current on the newest knowledge and the finest methods for handling dogs. To improve your talents, go to seminars, workshops, or courses.

In addition to providing dogs with physical control, effective dog handling involves making walks enjoyable and safe. These strategies guarantee the dogs in your care have a good and joyful time and establish a solid reputation in the dog walking sector.

Customer Service and Communication Skills

Having outstanding communication and customer service abilities is essential to the success of your dog-walking business. They support you in developing trusting bonds with customers, giving their dogs the finest care possible, and gaining recognition in the field. The following are some essential ideas and methods for honing these abilities:

1. Active Listening: When conversing with clients, engage in active listening. Observe their directions, preferences, and worries. This fosters trust and helps you comprehend their requirements more fully.
2. Clear Communication: Express yourself succinctly and clearly. Don't use technical terminology or jargon your clients might not comprehend; speak plainly. Make sure it's simple to follow your expectations and directions.
3. Responsiveness: React quickly to questions and concerns from customers. Promptly respond to texts, emails, and calls. Prompt replies demonstrate your regard for your customers and their animals.
4. Empathy: Be understanding and empathic with clients. Recognize their feelings and worries, particularly in emergency or stressful circumstances.
5. Professionalism: Ensure that you always conduct yourself with the utmost professionalism. This entails being on time, correctly attired, and projecting a professional image of yourself and your business.
6. Tailored Care: Provide every dog with individualized attention. Talk with the owner about the dog's unique

requirements and preferences so that you can adjust your services.

7. Clearly defined Policies and Contracts: Establish clearly defined policies and contracts. Ensure your clients understand your terms, prices, and unique circumstances. Make written agreements available for reference by both parties.
8. Client Education: Inform your clients about the safety and upkeep of dogs. Provide helpful information about behavior, health, and best practices for pets. Clients with knowledge are more inclined to respect your competence.
9. Resolving Complaints: Deal with grievances or issues promptly and professionally. As you hear the client's perspective, try to find a mutually agreeable solution or explanation.
10. Report and Updates: Frequently provide information on the dog's health and strolling experiences. Customers are informed and feel reassured by this.
11. Emergency Plans: Clearly define your emergency response strategy. Share this strategy with your clients so they know you are ready for unforeseen circumstances.

12. Privacy and Respect: Honor your clients' right to privacy. Don't divulge private information or dog pictures without permission. Keep things private.
13. Social Media: Share information on dog care and exciting material on social media and internet platforms. This can facilitate community building and client connections.
14. Customer input: Seek out and welcome client input. Consider their feedback to improve your services and solve any issues they may have.
15. Appreciation and Follow-Up: Express gratitude to customers for their business. Thank them for their faith in your services by sending follow-up communications or notes.
16. Training and Ongoing Education: Make educational and training investments in areas like communication and customer service. These abilities are just as crucial as your knowledge of dog care.
17. Managing Difficult Clients: Create plans for dealing with clients who are challenging or demanding. Problem-solving, patience, and attentive listening are useful in defusing difficult circumstances.

Excellent communication and customer service skills are essential to developing a devoted clientele and a successful dog-walking business. By prioritizing these abilities, you may build enduring client connections and give pets outstanding treatment.

Managing Difficult Situations and Client Concerns

In dog walking, you may occasionally encounter difficult circumstances and clients who have worries. How you manage these circumstances might significantly impact your reputation and your business's profitability. The following techniques can be used to address challenging circumstances and deal with customer concerns:

1. Remain Calm and Professional: Retain your professionalism and calm in the face of a challenging circumstance or a client's worries. Maintaining composure in the front of conflict facilitates the development of trust.
2. Active Listening: Pay close attention to what the customer has to say. Allow them to fully communicate their worries and refrain from interjecting. By actively listening, you show that you appreciate their opinions.

3. Empathize: Express understanding and empathy for the client's emotions and worries. Let them know you are aware of their feelings and that you are interested in finding a solution.
4. Deal with the Problem Quickly: Deal with the issue or worry as quickly as possible. Response times that are too long might exacerbate the issue and increase annoyance.
5. Collect Information: If the problem is associated with a particular occurrence, collect any pertinent data from your files, such as correspondence with the customer, notes, and photos.
6. Be Transparent: Communicate honestly and openly. Admit the mistake or misunderstanding and provide a remedy or clarification. Customers value openness and honesty.
7. Offer Sincere Apologies When Needed: If your dog walking service was at fault, extend your heartfelt apologies. Apologizing may be very helpful in settling disputes and preserving a good customer relationship.
8. Provide Solutions: Address the client's concerns with solutions. Offer solutions to resolve the issue and stop

it from happening again, such as a refund, extra services, or adjustments to your processes.

9. Follow-up: Once the problem has been resolved, contact the customer again to ensure they are happy with the arrangement. This helps restore confidence by demonstrating your dedication to their pleasure.
10. Make Changes: If the issue raises a recurrent problem, make the necessary adjustments to your training or processes to avoid reoccurring incidents.
11. Maintain Boundaries: Refrain from having heated or emotional conversations with customers when faced with difficult circumstances. Instead, keep your professional distance.
12. Record Incidents: Maintain a file of client complaints and your replies. Should the same problems recur in the future, this material may be helpful.
13. Seek Mediation: If you are unable to resolve a conflict with a challenging customer, you might want to think about bringing in an outsider, such as a mediator or trade association, to assist in mediating the issue.
14. Learn and Grow: Take advantage of difficult circumstances to further your career and personal development. Gain knowledge from every encounter

and keep refining your client interactions and offerings.

15. Legal Considerations: Know your legal rights and obligations as a dog walker, and when in doubt, get legal advice. It is crucial to have liability insurance and a well-written contract.
16. Termination as a Last Resort: You might have to consider parting ways with a troublesome customer in severe circumstances. But this needs to be done carefully and as a last option.

Managing challenging circumstances and customer problems in your dog walking business requires effective communication, critical thinking skills, and a dedication to client pleasure. You can safeguard the long-term survival of your organization, preserve excellent customer connections, and establish trust by properly and aggressively handling these difficulties.

Chapter 4: Getting Started - The Practical Side of Dog Walking

(Figure: 04)

Establishing a dog walking business is a thrilling endeavor combining your passion for animals and the chance to run your own business. Nonetheless, you must perform a few doable actions to launch your business and guarantee its success.

1. Legal Considerations: You must take care of your business's legal needs before you begin walking dogs. This includes registering your business, securing any licenses or permissions required, and researching local laws about pet services. You might also consider getting business insurance to safeguard yourself from mishaps or legal troubles.
2. Business Outline: Create a thorough business strategy that details your objectives, target market, price schedule, and promotional tactics. A carefully considered design will direct the expansion of your business and assist you in obtaining funds if necessary.
3. Marketing and Branding: You must sell your services and build a great brand to attract customers. This involves deciding on a catchy business name, creating a logo, developing a polished website, and using various marketing platforms, including local advertising, social media, and online directories.
4. Establishing Rates: Choose your dog walking service's price range. Examine the prices of your nearby rivals and consider variables like the number of dogs you want to walk, the length of the walks, and any other services you wish to provide.

5. Contracts and Agreements: To safeguard yourself and your clients, draft precise contracts, and service agreements. The services you'll offer, expectations, payment terms, and cancellation policies should all be included in these contracts.
6. Equipment and materials: Purchase the gear required for walking dogs, such as first aid kits, waste bags, leashes, and harnesses. Making sure you have high-quality equipment is essential for the dogs' well-being and safety.
7. Record-keeping: Establish a procedure for maintaining records. This entails keeping track of payments according to timetables and recording all dog's unique requirements and behaviors.
8. Safety and Readiness: Assemble the skills and information necessary for first aid, emergency response, and dog behavior. This preparation guarantees your ability to manage a range of scenarios with ease.
9. Client Onboarding: It's critical to offer a seamless onboarding experience to your first clients. Meet them to review their dog's requirements, inclinations, and

unique guidelines. Create a trusting impression right away.

10. Scheduling and Time Management: Create effective scheduling procedures to guarantee that you can accommodate several clients' demands while controlling your workload. Effective time management is vital in this line of work.
11. Socialization and Compatibility: Make sure the dogs you intend to walk together are compatible and well-socialized. This reduces the possibility of disputes during strolls.
12. Client contact: Keep lines of communication with your clients open and transparent. Give frequent updates on their dog's health and be reachable in case of inquiries or worries. Establishing long-term relationships and fostering trust depends on effective client communication.
13. Growth Strategies: Make plans for your business's future expansion. As your firm grows, think about adding more dog walkers, adding more services, or going after new markets.

Launching a dog walking business requires careful preparation, perseverance, and dedication to the welfare of the dogs entrusted to your care. Maintaining organization and addressing practical issues can help you build a profitable business and have a rewarding career working with these cherished creatures.

Equipment and Supplies You'll Need

To guarantee the security and welfare of the dogs in your care, you'll need the appropriate tools and materials to operate a profitable dog-walking business. The following is a list of necessities:

1. Leashes: Invest in long-lasting, premium leashes in various lengths to suit diverse walking conditions. Although a regular 6-foot leash is quite flexible, there are situations when you'll want a shorter or longer one.
2. Collars or Harnesses: Select the proper collars or harnesses based on the dog's breed, size, and temperament. Harnesses are frequently recommended since they offer greater control and lessen the pressure on the dog's neck.
3. Waste Bags: Always take waste bags to clean up after the dogs after walks. Consider the environment by utilizing biodegradable bags.

4. First Aid Kit: When caring for minor wounds or crises on a stroll, a kit designed specifically for pets is necessary. Ensure it has gauze, tweezers, bandages, and antiseptic wipes.
5. Water and a portable bowl: Always have water on hand, especially for extended hikes in hot weather. Hydrating the dogs is made easier with a foldable water bowl.
6. Goodies and Rewards: Good behavior is boosted by using goodies as reinforcement. These can guarantee the dogs have a good experience and aid in training.
7. Poop Scoop or Pooper Scooper: A scoop or scooper helps collect dog poop and tidy the area around a walking path.
8. Dog Identification Tags: Ensure all dogs in your care have appropriate tags that provide the owner's contact details. These may be helpful when a dog gets lost while on a stroll.
9. Pet First Aid and CPR Manual: A manual or reference book on pet first aid and CPR techniques might be helpful in an emergency.

10. Whistle or Clicker: These tools can help with dog training and communication. These resources are beneficial for memory training.
11. Multi-Tool or Swiss Army Knife: During hikes, a multi-tool with several uses, such as a knife and scissors, can be helpful in various activities.
12. Flashlight or Headlamp: A flashlight or headlamp can increase safety and visibility while walking dogs after dark or in low light.
13. Mobile Phone: Always keep a mobile phone with you for client communication, emergencies, and route finding.
14. Dog ID and Behavior Profile: Every dog needs a card that includes their photo, the owner's contact information, and information on their behavior, special requirements, and allergies.
15. Maps and Routes: Learn the walking routes and local maps so that you may organize enjoyable and safe outings. GPS applications might also be helpful to ensure you don't get lost and track your path.
16. Waste Disposal Container: Store spent waste bags in a container or bag until you have a suitable place to dispose of them.

17. Business Cards: Keep a supply of business cards on hand to give to prospective customers or anybody who asks about your offerings.
18. Pet Camera or GPS Tracker (Optional): Some dog walkers utilize pet webcams or GPS trackers to monitor their dogs' whereabouts and conduct while walking. Clients may feel more secure and at ease as a result.
19. Business Uniform or Logo Apparel (Optional): If you want to look more put together and noticeable while working, think about donning a uniform or branded clothing.

For the dogs you walk to be comfortable, safe, and have a positive overall experience, you must have the proper supplies and equipment. Be organized, well-prepared, and equipped to handle any issue that may come up when you take your dogs for walks. Your clients will value your expertise and commitment to the welfare of their animals.

Pricing Your Services and Fee Structures

Your dog walking business must choose the appropriate price structure to be financially successful and competitive. While determining your service prices, keep the following things in mind:

1. Market research: To start, gather information about local price patterns through market research. Find out how much other dog walkers are charging for comparable services. You may use this as a starting point to determine your pricing.
2. Service Type: Consider the kinds of services you want to provide. Do you offer regular walks to dogs, walks in groups, or specific services like socialization for puppies or care for older dogs? Pricing for different services may vary.
3. Length of Walks: Choose how long your typical walks will be. Walks lasting one hour usually cost more than walks lasting thirty, although the cost should be reasonable for the area.
4. Number of Dogs: Consider how walking more than one dog at once may impact your charges. Walking more than one dog from the same home may incur additional fees from confident dog walkers.
5. Other Services: Consider providing additional services like pet sitting, transportation, or overnight care.

Packages or separate prices may apply to these services.

6. Location and Accessibility: Your dog walking business's site may impact the prices you charge. You might be able to set more if you live in a busy urban region with solid demand. Furthermore, your pricing could align with where your services are more easily accessible, such as near a park.
7. Costs and expenditures: Determine the fees and expenses of your pet care business, including marketing, insurance, administrative overhead, transportation, and pet care equipment. You should be able to profit and pay these expenditures with your price.
8. Profit Margin: Establish the desired profit margin. Strive to balance maintaining your business's financial viability and being competitive.
9. Demand for Your Services: Consider the extent to which your services are in need in your locality. You might be able to charge more if you have a loyal customer base and a backlog.
10. Competitive Positioning: Think about how you stand out in the industry. Do you present as an inexpensive

alternative or provide upscale, customized services? Pricing needs to be in line with the market positioning you have selected.

11. Value-Added Services: You can charge more by providing value-added services like behavior instruction while on walks, updates, or pet report cards.
12. Seasonal Pricing: Consider changing your prices according to the season, for example, around holidays or during the busiest travel periods when demand could be more significant.
13. Bundles and Discounts: Provide price bundles for customers who schedule your services frequently or ahead of time discounts. This may encourage sustained dedication.
14. Perceived Value: Recognize the value your clients believe you provide. Your dependability, professionalism, and level of service quality enhance the value you offer.
15. Customer Feedback: Consider what customers have to say about your prices. If customers say your prices are too high, consider lowering them. In a similar vein, if customers continuously compliment your offerings,

this may mean that your current rates are reasonable or warrant raising them.

16. Contract and Payment Conditions: Clearly state in your service agreements or contracts what your payment conditions are. This covers the payment method (cash, credit card, or Internet), invoicing frequency (weekly or monthly), and late fees.

Determining the appropriate price structure for your dog walking business takes balance. It must consider the local market, pay your costs, yield a respectable profit margin, and complement the specialization and positioning of your business. To stay competitive and reach your financial objectives, regularly assess your price, and make any necessary adjustments.

Creating Service Packages

Offering service packages to customers can help your dog walking business grow both in terms of clientele and retention. You may accommodate your clients' varying demands and tastes by providing a range of packages. Here's how to develop and promote service bundles:

1. Evaluate Client Needs: Start by learning about the requirements and inclinations of your possible customers. While some people like daily walks, others

might want more specialized or infrequent services like elderly dog walks, puppy care, or pet transportation.

2. Service Differentiation: Make your services stand out by designing packages that address various requirements. Think of the length of the walk, solo or group walks, the time of day, and any other services you may provide.
3. Price Structure: Establish the cost of every product. Verify that it accurately represents the cost of the rendered services. The type of service, its duration, and any extras can all affect the price.
4. Bundle Names: Make sure the names of each bundle are memorable and informative. Packages with words like "Adventure Walks," "Puppy Playtime," or "Senior Dog Strolls" are more likely to catch people's attention.
5. Services Provided: Clearly state the contents of each package. Indicate the length of the walks, the frequency of the walks, any extra services (such as pet sitting or transportation), and any special features of the package.
6. Personalization: Provide your packages with a certain level of personalization. To better meet their dog's

demands, clients may change the frequency or length of their walks.

7. Loyalty and Bulk Discounts: Consider providing customers who commit to longer-term packages or multiple services with discounts or loyalty benefits. This may promote keeping customers.
8. Seasonal or Promotional Packages: Develop seasonal or promotional packages to draw customers at particular periods of the year or to draw attention to exclusive deals. For example, you may offer a "Holiday Walks" package throughout the holiday season.
9. Marketing Materials: To advertise your packages, create marketing materials. This entails adding comprehensive information about each package to your brochures, social media accounts, and website.
10. Client Consultation: Help clients select the package that best meets their dog's needs by reviewing the various options with them during the consultation. Stress the benefits and ease of use of bundle offers.
11. Transparent Pricing: Make sure that your prices are open and understandable. It should be simple for clients to comprehend how much each bundle costs and what they are getting in return.

12. Customer Feedback: Find out what customers think of your service offerings. Over time, use this input to enhance and improve your offers.
13. Client Onboarding: Help new customers select the package that best suits their demands and budget by outlining the many options.
14. Consistent Service Delivery: Provide the services that are part of every package consistently. Make sure customers get the quality and worth they anticipate.
15. Review and Modify: Consistently assess how well your service packages are performing. Make adjustments in response to customer feedback, shifts in demand, and market competition.

For your dog walking business, offering service packages might draw in a more extensive clientele and provide a steadier flow of revenue. You may deliver first-rate service and create enduring customer connections by providing well-crafted packages that address various client demands.

Developing a Scheduling System

excellent management of your dog-walking business requires a perfect scheduling system. It ensures you can continue to manage your workload and satisfy your client's expectations. Here's how to create a scheduling plan:

1. Digital Scheduling Software: Make an investment in programs or software for scheduling that are made especially for dog-walking companies. These programs provide features including appointment scheduling, client management, and automated reminders. Time To Pet, Pet Sitter Plus, and Paw Loyalty are well-liked choices.
2. Centralized Calendar: Keep an up-to-date, centralized calendar that lets you quickly view all your appointments and schedules. This keeps you from making duplicate reservations and guarantees effective time management.
3. Client Information Database: Establish a client database with information on the client's breed, name of dog, behavior notes, and preferred timetables, among other things. This database makes it simpler to match customer requests with open time slots.
4. Online Booking: Using your website or scheduling software, allow your clients to make online reservations. This eliminates the need for back-and-

forth communication by making it easier for clients to request appointments.

5. Time Blocks: Assign time slots to your workday according to the services you provide, the number of dogs you can walk at once, and the time it takes you to go between appointments. This facilitates effective time management.
6. Clearly State Your Availability: Clearly state your working hours and availability. This includes indicating if you are employed on the weekends, holidays, and specific times.
7. Buffer Time: Plan for any unforeseen delays or make sure you don't rush between walks by adding extra time between appointments. By doing this, you may reduce tension and preserve the caliber of your service.
8. Preferred Client Schedules: Maintain a record of recurrent clients' preferred schedules. It can improve their experience to have this information easily accessible as some clients might choose walks during particular times.
9. Communication System: Establish a system for automatically sending clients updates, reminders, and

confirmations of appointments. This can lower last-minute cancellations and no-shows.

10. Mobile Accessibility: You can access your scheduling system from a mobile device if you need to review or alter schedules while on the road.
11. Cancellation and Rescheduling Policy: Make sure there is a clear policy for cancellations and rescheduling, including any necessary costs and requirements for prior notice. Share this policy with your clientele.
12. Waitlist function: To notify clients when an appointment becomes available because of a cancellation, consider creating a waitlist function if your demand is strong.
13. Holiday and Special Occasion Schedules: Establish precise timetables and notify clients of any modifications or limitations to prepare for holidays and special events.
14. Regular examination: To find any inefficiencies or potential areas for development, examine your scheduling system regularly. Constantly adjust to the changing demands of your business.
15. Schedule Downtime: Schedule some time for relaxation and rejuvenation. Steer clear of

overbooking, which can result in burnout and worse service.

An efficient scheduling system is essential to a dog-walking business's success. It enables you to manage your time effectively, balance the demands of your clients, and deliver a consistent level of service. You may streamline your scheduling process and concentrate on giving the pets in your care exceptional care if you have the appropriate policies and procedures.

Insurance and Liability Protection

Ensuring your dog walking business is adequately insured and has liability coverage to preserve your assets and industry is essential. These are crucial insurance choices to think about:

1. General Liability Insurance: This type of insurance protects you if you are involved in an accident or sustain injuries while walking your dog. It can shield you from legal action if a dog in your care hurts a person or animal or if you cause damage to someone's property while on a walk.
2. Professional Liability Insurance: Also referred to as errors and omissions insurance, this type of coverage can shield you if a customer alleges that you caused

them injury or financial loss. This might involve problems with pet care, carelessness, or contract disagreements.

3. Insurance for Care, Custody, and Control (CCC): CCC insurance is exclusive to those who perform pet care services, such as dog walkers. It protects against harm, disease, and death to animals under your care. This kind of coverage is essential to shield you from liabilities about the dogs themselves.
4. Commercial Property Insurance: Consider purchasing commercial property insurance if your dog walking business has a physical location, such as an office or storage facility. It covers harm to your business's assets, such as furniture, supplies, and machinery.
5. Workers' Compensation Insurance: Workers' compensation insurance can be necessary in your location if you use independent contractors or have employees. It offers coverage for diseases or injuries your workers may have.
6. Firm Interruption Insurance: If a covered event, such as a natural disaster or property damage, renders your firm temporarily unable to operate, business

interruption insurance can assist in restoring lost revenue and cover expenditures.

7. Commercial Auto Insurance: Ensure that your car is covered by commercial auto insurance if you use it for dog walking services. This coverage covers damage and accidents from operating a vehicle for commercial purposes.
8. Umbrella Liability Insurance: In addition to the limits of your other policies, an umbrella policy offers additional liability coverage. In the event of significant litigation or claims that exceed your primary coverage, it may provide additional protection.
9. Cyber Liability Insurance: Cyber liability insurance can shield you from data breaches, cyberattacks, and privacy violations if you store sensitive client information electronically.
10. Pet Sitters Bonds: Dog walkers and pet sitters may be required by certain states or local authorities to obtain a pet sitters bond. This bond acts as an assurance of the professionalism and accountability of your business.
11. Legal and Regulatory Compliance: Ensure you know local insurance laws or regulations. Adherence to local

legislation is imperative to avert legal complications and preserve liability protection.

12. Risk Management and Safety Protocols: To reduce the possibility of mishaps and legal concerns, put safety protocols and risk management techniques into practice. Some examples include comprehensive pet assessments, client communication, and safe handling techniques.
13. Please speak with an Insurance Professional: You should talk with an insurance broker or professional specializing in small businesses and pet care. They can help you assess your needs and find the right insurance policies for your dog-walking business.

Before selecting insurance coverage, carefully review policy terms, limits, deductibles, and exclusions. Ensure that your chosen insurance provider is reputable and has a good track record of handling claims. Appropriate insurance and liability protection gives you peace of mind and safeguard your business in unexpected incidents or legal disputes.

Chapter 5: Marketing and Building Your Brand

(Figure: 05)

Building a successful dog-walking business requires a strong marketing and branding strategy. Here are some tips for developing a powerful brand and advertising your services:

1. Create an Online Presence: An online presence is essential in our digital world. Make a polished website highlighting your offerings, costs, and customer reviews. Utilize beautiful images of content dogs to add interest and appeal to your website. Create profiles on social media sites like LinkedIn, Facebook, and Instagram to communicate with possible customers and attract a wider audience.
2. Use social media: Dog walkers may effectively promote themselves through social media. Share updates, pictures, and videos from your dog walking trips on these networks. Talk to your audience by answering their questions and remarks. Post educational and amusing articles on dog care to establish your authority in the area.
3. Content marketing: Start a blog or make educational films and articles about training, behavior, and other dog-related subjects. In addition to drawing in new customers, content marketing highlights your proficiency with dog walking and other pet care tasks.
4. Local SEO: Ensure your web material is optimized for local search engines (SEO). This ensures that when prospective customers look for dog walkers in your

region, your business comes up in local search results. Ensure your business is listed on directories such as Google My Business and incorporate local keywords into the text of your website.

5. Testimonials from Customers: Invite pleased customers to provide evaluations and comments on your website and other review platforms. Positive testimonials from satisfied customers might greatly influence decisions made by prospective clients.
6. Networking: Connect with nearby veterinary clinics, pet groomers, and other companies catering to pet owners. These specialists' recommendations might be a wonderful way to get new clients. To promote these collaborations, consider providing incentives for referrals.
7. Community Engagement: Take part in pet-related local activities, fairs, and get-togethers. This is a great chance to network with possible clients and show them how much you love dogs and care for their welfare.
8. Uniforms and Branding: Invest in business-related branded clothing or uniforms bearing your business name and logo. When customers see you in uniform, it

strengthens your brand and fosters a reputation for dependability and trust.

9. Business Cards and Brochures: Be prepared to provide prospective customers with business cards and brochures. These documents must contain your services, contact details, and a brief business overview.
10. Special Offers and Promotions: Draw in new customers by providing exclusive promos like free initial walks or incentives for referring others. Promotions may help generate interest in your business and persuade customers to try you out.
11. Consistency and Reliability: Offering dependable, consistent service is essential to developing a good brand. Keep lines of communication open with customers, deliver high-quality service, and be on time for appointments. Your brand and reputation are based on your interactions with your clients.
12. Differentiation: Emphasize what makes your dog walking business unique from the others. Highlight your distinctive qualities, such as your training, expertise, particular services, or commitment to the pets.

13. Gather and Disseminate Tales: Gather touching anecdotes and tales from your dog walks, then post them on your website and social media. These narratives can emotionally engage and establish trust with prospective customers.

Developing your brand and marketing your dog walking business takes time and work. To establish a good reputation and draw in customers who respect your services, you must be consistent, professional, and have a sincere affection for dogs. Your brand will eventually be associated with superior dog care in your neighborhood.

Creating a Professional Website and Social Media Presence

Your dog-walking business must have a strong web presence in the digital era. Here's how to make an eye-catching social media presence and a polished website:

Business Website:

1. Domain Name and Hosting: Register a domain corresponding to your organization's name or services. Select a trustworthy hosting business to guarantee the dependability and speed of your website.
2. Expert Design: Invest in a website designed by a professional. The layout should be clear, easy to use,

and represent the essence of your business. Make use of gorgeous photos of canines and your offerings.

3. Unambiguous Navigation: Establish a user-friendly navigation framework. Ensure that important information, such as services, costs, contact information, and customer reviews, is easily accessible to visitors.
4. Educational Content: Give thorough details about your dog walking services, such as service descriptions, costs, experience and background, and any special deals you may have. To become recognized as an authority in the industry, provide insightful articles about dog behavior, care, and training.
5. Testimonials and Reviews: Prominently display client endorsements and reviews on your website. Positive testimonies from content consumers foster confidence in prospective clients.
6. Contact Information: Provide your phone number, email address, and contact form clearly and understandably to facilitate simple questions. Provide a map of the area you service.

7. Blog: Establish a blog on your website and post dog-related content regularly. This aids in search engine optimization (SEO) and offers helpful information.
8. Online Booking: Provide clients with the opportunity to book online, if applicable. Your services may become more attractive due to this ease.
9. SEO Optimization: Employ pertinent keywords and metadata to enhance your website's search engine optimization (SEO). When prospective customers look for dog walking services in your region, this raises the ranking of your website in search results.
10. Mobile-Friendly: Considering how many people use smartphones and tablets to access the internet, ensure your website is adaptable to smaller screens. A website optimized for mobile devices improves user experience.
11. Legal and Privacy Policies: Ensure your website has explicit legal and privacy policies. Customers must be informed about how their data is handled, and you must take legal precautions to safeguard your business.

Online Social Presence:

1. Platform Selection: Decide which social media sites are most appropriate for your intended audience. Dog-walking companies frequently use Facebook, Instagram, and Twitter.
2. Consistent Branding: Make sure your social media profiles have the same branding. Use your business's colors, typefaces, and logo to establish a unified design.
3. Engaging information: Distribute exciting details, such as pictures and videos of the dogs you walk, educational articles about grooming dogs, and updates about your offerings. Encourage engagement from your viewers by leaving likes, comments, and shares.
4. Posting Timetable: Establish a regular posting timetable. Posting often and on schedule keeps readers interested and informed.
5. Reply to Comments: Interact with your audience by immediately answering messages and comments. Promote dialogue while delivering top-notch client support.
6. Hashtags: Include pertinent hashtags in your postings to make your material more visible to a broader audience.

7. Stories and Live Videos: Use tools like Facebook Live and Instagram Stories to provide behind-the-scenes videos and real-time updates. This might help you establish a more intimate relationship with your viewers.
8. Promotions and competitions: Occasionally hold social media competitions or promotions to encourage participation and draw in new followers.
9. Community Involvement: Highlight your activities within the neighborhood's dog- and pet-loving community. Talk about your involvement in local business collaborations, charitable endeavors, and events.
10. Advertising: To target particular demographics in your service region, use paid advertising on social media networks.

Analytics: You may monitor the effectiveness of your postings by using social media analytics. You may improve your social media presence and your content strategy with the aid of this data.

A solid social media presence and an informative website are crucial for growing your dog-walking business's clientele. To persuade prospective consumers that you're the most excellent option for their cherished pets, your internet presence should demonstrate the caliber, professionalism, and enthusiasm you provide for your services.

Building a Strong Online Portfolio

An online portfolio may effectively market your dog walking service, emphasize your experience, and win over new clients. Here's how to build a robust internet portfolio:

1. Platform Selection: Decide which platform to house your online portfolio. Some options include your business website, websites devoted to your portfolio, or social networking sites like Facebook or Instagram.
2. Professional Presentation: Make sure the style of your web portfolio is tidy and expert. Take advantage of a logical color palette, sharp photos, and an easy-to-use structure.
3. Excellent Photography: Provide amazing, well-groomed photographs of dogs you have walked, pet care scenarios, and contented pets. Your degree of care and attention should be reflected in your photos.

4. Service Descriptions: Describe the service you were delivering, the dogs participating, and any unique characteristics of the walk-in photo or set of images.
5. Testimonials from Clients: Include client endorsements and evaluations. These recommendations provide your portfolio more legitimacy and serve as social confirmation of the caliber of your services.
6. Variety of Dogs: To show that you can adapt to different personalities and demands, provide a portfolio with various dogs and breeds.
7. Action photos: Add photos showing the pups' enthusiasm and vigor while walking. These pictures capture the happiness you bring to your work.
8. Calm and peaceful Moments: To show that you can give the dogs in your care a secure and relaxing environment, balance activity images with quiet moments.
9. Professionalism: Use photos of your equipment, your clients, and their dogs, and your uniform or branded clothing to emphasize professionalism.

10. Diverse Environments: You can walk dogs in various settings, including parks, cities, and undeveloped paths. This illustrates how flexible you are.
11. Before-and-After Pictures: To demonstrate your skill, provide before-and-after pictures if you've worked with behavior training clients or significantly influenced a dog's behavior.
12. Playful and engaging Moments: Document lighthearted and engaging moments with the canines to demonstrate your capacity to build a close bond with them.
13. Detailed Descriptions: Compose thorough explanations for every image or set of ideas. Describe the circumstances, the dog's actions, and your assistance.
14. Contact Details: Make sure your portfolio has your contact details in an accessible location so prospective customers can contact you.
15. Shareable Content: Ensure your portfolio is readily shared using direct links or social media icons. Urge pleased customers to forward your portfolio to their contacts.

16. Consistency: Update your portfolio with the most recent pieces of work. Add fresh images and stories regularly to demonstrate that your business is growing and operating.
17. Keyword Optimization: Ensure your descriptions and captions contain essential keywords related to dog walking services. This can increase search engines' ability to find your portfolio.
18. Privacy and Consent: Ensure you have your client's permission before including their pets or other personally identifiable information in your portfolio. Be mindful of confidentiality and privacy.

A visual depiction of your abilities and the caliber of care you give canines may be seen in your web portfolio. You may enhance your chances of drawing in new business and establishing credibility with prospective customers by presenting your work expertly and captivatingly.

Networking in Your Local Pet Community

One of the best ways to expand your dog walking business is to establish a strong network among the local pet community. Here's how to create and preserve meaningful relationships:

1. Participate in Local Pet activities: Participate in pet-related activities, such as adoption fairs, pet expos, or charity fundraisers, in your town. Meeting other pet experts and owners is a terrific opportunity at these events.
2. Join Pet Groups: Consider Becoming a member of neighborhood pet-related groups or associations. These clubs frequently hold meetings, activities, and networking opportunities for their members.
3. Volunteer at Shelters: As an opportunity to give back to the community, volunteering at animal shelters or rescue groups also fosters professional and pet-loving relationships.
4. Work Together with vets: Establish connections with nearby vets. Both you and they may refer customers to them for their pet's medical needs and your dog walking business.
5. Make Connections with Pet Groomers: Groomers frequently engage with pet owners and can know of individuals who might benefit from dog walking services. Make contact with nearby pet groomers.
6. Collaborate with Pet Stores: Reach out to local pet retailers. In exchange for promoting their goods or

services to your customers, you can leave business cards or brochures at their locations.

7. Participate on social media: Actively participate on social media platforms in local pet-related groups and sites. Engage with pet owners who could require your services by sharing your knowledge.
8. Visit Dog Parks: Go to your neighborhood dog park and talk to the dog owners there. Distribute flyers or business cards and inform them about your offerings.
9. Establish an Online Presence: Keep a robust online presence, encompassing a website and social media accounts, enabling you to interact with prospective customers and the neighborhood pet community.
10. Organize Workshops or Seminars: Consider organizing workshops or seminars on training or dog care subjects. By doing this, you may draw in clients and position yourself as an authority in your industry.
11. Provide Referral Incentives: Give current customers discounts or other prizes to get them to recommend you to their friends and family.
12. Partnerships with Pet-Related Businesses: Work together with other nearby pet-related companies. For instance, work with a pet photographer to provide

joint advertisements or a pet trainer to provide packages of services.

13. Attend City Council Meetings: Attend any city council or local government meetings addressing pet regulations. You may maintain your connection to the neighborhood pet community by being aware and active in these conversations.
14. Participate in Local Pet Forums: In discussion boards or local pet forums where pet owners exchange suggestions, guidance, and tips. Provide insightful commentary and, where appropriate, advertise your services.
15. Get Involved: Participate in or support neighborhood gatherings that include pets, dog parades, or charity walks. Community involvement shows that you care about pets and their welfare.

Establishing a solid network within the local pet community takes time and commitment, but the benefits to your dog walking business may be enormous. Building connections and interacting with professionals, pet owners, and pet-related groups can help you grow your clientele and build a solid reputation in your neighborhood.

Effective Advertising and Marketing Strategies

Consider these advertising and marketing techniques to effectively advertise your dog walking service and draw in more customers:

1. Local SEO: Make sure your website is optimized for local search engines. Use location-specific content and keywords to raise your website's profile in local search results.
2. Google My Business: Establish and enhance your listing on Google My Business. It is essential for local exposure. Ensure all your business's information is correct, including your address, phone number, and operating hours.
3. Social Media Marketing: Connect with your neighborhood using social media sites like Facebook, Instagram, and Twitter. Post engaging content such as pictures and videos of your dog walks, enlightening pet care advice, and customer endorsements.
4. Pay-Per-Click (PPC) Advertising: Use Facebook and Google Ads for PPC advertising campaigns. These can assist you in attracting visitors to your website and targeting particular local demographics.

5. Content Marketing: Establish a blog on your website and provide educational articles on issues about dogs, training, and other pet-related subjects regularly. This raises the search engine rating of your website while showcasing your skills.
6. Email marketing: Create a database of previous and prospective customers' emails. Distribute newsletters that include promotions, updates, and insightful articles. Maintaining communication with your audience through email marketing works well.
7. Referral Program: Establish a program that motivates your present clientele to recommend new consumers. Provide discounts or prizes as a means of encouraging practical recommendations.
8. Flyers and Brochures: Create and hand out flyers and brochures in neighborhood dog parks, veterinary offices, pet shops, and other public spaces. Make sure they include a prominent call to action and eye-catching graphics.
9. Local Business Partnerships: Work together with other nearby companies that cater to pets, such as pet shops, groomers, and vets. Increase your reach by promoting each other's services together.

10. Online Testimonials and Reviews: Motivate happy customers to post reviews on Facebook, Yelp, and Google. Favorable evaluations increase prospective clients' trust.
11. Networking: Join pet-related groups and go to local pet events. Connecting with pet owners and other veterinary experts might result in collaborations and recommendations.
12. Promote in Local Media: Consider promoting in regional radio, magazines, and newspapers. You may reach a large audience in your neighborhood with the aid of local media.
13. Public Relations: Compose news releases detailing your business's accomplishments and any significant events. For possible coverage, please submit them to your community's media sources.
14. Vehicle Branding: Put your business name, logo, and contact details on your dog-walking vehicle. This mobile advertising may prompt questions from onlookers.
15. Special Offers and Specials: Occasionally, unique specials, such as first-time customer discounts or

seasonal sales. Promotions have the power to draw in new clients and boost recurring revenue.

16. Perform Community Service: Showcase your dedication to the neighborhood by participating in fundraising activities or providing dog walking services to nearby animal shelters or rescue groups.
17. Analyze and modify consistently assess how well your marketing initiatives work. Examine which marketing tactics attract the most customers, then modify your strategy appropriately.

Online and offline marketing initiatives are part of a comprehensive marketing plan for your dog walking business. By implementing these tactics, you may reach a larger audience, create a powerful online presence, and develop a devoted clientele. Recall that in the pet care sector, word-of-mouth referrals, consistently high standards of service, and consistency are effective marketing strategies.

Handling Customer Testimonials and Reviews

Client testimonials and reviews greatly aid in building trust and drawing in new customers for your dog walking service. Here's how to deal with and take advantage of them:

1. Promote Reviews: Inspire testimonials and reviews from your pleased customers. Tell them you value their input and how it advances your business.
2. Select the Correct Platforms: Pay attention to well-known review sites like Google, Yelp, Facebook, and websites particular to your sector like Wag or Rover. Ensure all your business profiles on these sites are accurate and complete.
3. React Quickly: Quickly address reviews, both favorable and unfavorable. This indicates your dedication to providing excellent customer service.
4. Be Professional and Polite: Even if a review is unfavorable, you should still respond professionally and courteously. When required, provide an explanation or a solution in response to the feedback.
5. Express Thanks to Positive Reviewers: Express gratitude to customers who write positive reviews for support and selecting your services. Saying "thank you" is adequate.
6. Handle Unfavorable evaluations: Take inadequate evaluations as a chance to do better. Address the

issues raised, provide an explanation or a remedy, and reaffirm your dedication to providing top-notch service.

7. Preserve Confidentiality: When replying to reviews, refrain from disclosing sensitive or private customer information. Observe client privacy and confidentiality.
8. Emphasize favorable Feedback: Use endorsements and good evaluations for your website, social media accounts, and promotional materials. Emphasize the most insightful and thorough comments.
9. Share Success Tales: Create success tales out of happy client encounters. Write blog entries or case studies on difficult or touching circumstances where your services were helpful.
10. Show Reviews on Your Website: You may use widgets or separate pages to display reviews. Your internet presence gains credibility and social proof as a result.
11. Use Video Testimonials: Request customer testimonials; they may be much more compelling and convincing than textual evaluations.
12. Use Reviews in Marketing: Use brief quotes from favorable reviews in your brochures, posters, and

social media postings. Showcase them to prospective customers to demonstrate the caliber of your offerings.

13. Post Review Snippets on social media: Post brief reviews on your social media accounts to expand your reach and remind your existing followers of the positive experiences your customers have had.
14. Establish a Strategy for Gathering Reviews: • Create a systematic strategy for gathering reviews, such as asking for comments on specific platforms or following up with emails following a service.
15. Check Review Sites: Keep an eye out for fresh comments regularly. Establish alerts or notifications so you can keep informed and react quickly.
16. Get Permission: To protect your client's privacy, get their consent before utilizing their complete names, pictures, or video testimonies.
17. Preserve Transparency: When managing reviews, transparency is essential. If you come across a less-than-stellar review, be sure to manage it in a professional yet transparent manner.

The legitimacy and reputation of your dog walking service may be significantly increased by managing client testimonials and reviews well. You can establish trust with present and future customers by proactively responding to comments and highlighting your dedication to exceptional customer service.

Chapter 6: Building and Managing Client Relationships

(Figure: 06)

The foundation of your dog walking business is your clientele. You may build a devoted customer base and guarantee repeat business by fostering these relationships:

1. Clear Communication: Establishing client connections requires effective communication. Ensure your kind, accommodating, and ready to answer their queries and concerns throughout the process, from the initial consultation to routine updates on their dogs. Maintaining regular contact builds faith in your abilities.
2. Tailored Service: Each pet and customer are different. Customize your offerings to each client's unique requirements and the character of their pets. By providing individualized care, you show that you are committed to their furry family members' pleasure and well-being.
3. Consistency and Reliability: Maintain a consistent level of quality and dependability in your services. Establishing and maintaining regular schedules, being punctual for walks, and offering excellent care give your clients peace of mind and a sense of assurance that their dogs are in capable hands.
4. Adaptability and Flexibility: Recognize that clients' demands and schedules could alter. Adjust and change as needed to meet their changing needs. Customers like your flexibility in meeting their needs.

5. Transparent Pricing and Policies: It's critical that pricing and corporate policies be made evident. Customers must know your prices, cancelation procedures, and extra costs. Building trust begins with honest and sincere discussion about these issues.
6. Professionalism and Reliability: Keep your look, manner, and work ethic professional. Demonstrate your dependability and that you take your obligations seriously. Two essential elements of trust are dependability and professionalism.
7. Follow-Up and Feedback: Ensure clients are happy with your services by contacting them after each walk or service. Ask for input, pay attention to their recommendations, or worries, and act quickly to resolve them. This demonstrates your appreciation for their feedback and your dedication to ongoing development.
8. Loyalty Programs and Special Offers: Provide promotional offers, exclusive discounts, or loyalty programs for recurring customers. Rewarding their loyalty keeps them around longer and motivates them to recommend your services to others.

9. The Human-Pet Bond: Create a personal connection with the animals you look after. Learn about their distinct inclinations, actions, and personalities. In addition to helping the pets, this relationship gives consumers peace of mind that their animals are getting love and care.
10. Managing Issues with Grace: There will inevitably be worries or problems. When these circumstances come up, manage them professionally and with grace. Provide answers, accept accountability when necessary, and make sure the client feels understood and appreciated.
11. Celebrate Special Occasions: Recall and honor your pet's life milestones, such as birthdays or adoption anniversaries. Establishing a personal connection with your clients may be significantly enhanced by sending them a short card or message.
12. Keep Up to Date: Remain updated on pet care trends, industry best practices, and any new developments about dog walking. Customers value your dedication to being current with pet care innovations.
13. Surprise and Delight: Occasionally, surprise your clients with tiny gifts, such as a handwritten message

of gratitude or a picture of their contented dog after a walk. These little surprises strengthen your connections.

14. Secrecy and Personal Space: Be discreet and considerate of the privacy of your clients. Don't divulge any client information or pet-related facts without authorization.

Building strong client relationships is a continuous process that needs commitment and consideration. You can establish enduring relationships with your clients and ensure their loyalty and the welfare of their dogs by offering excellent service, being approachable, and putting a personal touch on things.

The Initial Consultation Process

Consultation is essential to building a fruitful and reliable connection with your clients. This is how the procedure is broken down:

1. Setting Up the Meeting: Set up a time for the consultation that works for you and the client to start. These sessions are usually best held in person, but they can also be controlled via phone or video conference if that is not possible.

2. Getting Ready for the Gathering: Make a list of what you need to address and the questions you want to ask before the appointment. This includes learning about the client's pet, needs, and unique demands or worries.
3. Introduction and Establishing a Good rapport: Introduce yourself and your dog walking business to start the encounter. Establish a relationship with the customer by showing sincere interest in their pet and unique needs.
4. Talking About Creature Details: Learn everything there is to know about the creature you want to walk, such as its breed, age, health history, nutritional requirements, and any peculiarities in its behavior. You can better customize your services the more you understand about the pet.
5. Comprehending the customer's Expectations: Find out from the customer what they anticipate, such as how often they want to walk their pet, which routes they like, and if they have any special instructions. It is essential to comprehend their wants to offer a personalized service.
6. Safety and Health Issues: Talk about safety and health issues. Ensure the pet has received all recommended

vaccines, and find out about any allergies, illnesses, or prescriptions the pet could need while in your care.

7. Routine and Behavior: Find out about the pet's preferred form of exercise, daily schedule, and any behavioral issues. Knowing their habits and behavior makes providing the pet a pleasant and pleasurable experience easier.
8. Emergency Contacts and Key Exchange: Get the client's emergency contact details in case you cannot contact them. Talk about exchanging keys or establishing entrance procedures for the client's house and set rules about pet access.
9. Provide a thorough service agreement that covers all the specifics of your dog walking services, such as costs, availability, cancellation procedures, and liabilities. Make sure the customer understands the conditions and that you both agree to them.
10. Handling Questions and Concerns: Invite the customer to share any queries or worries. Be ready to discuss things honestly and appropriately.
11. Client and Pet Compatibility: Evaluate whether your services and the demands of the pet are compatible. If

it's clear that your services aren't the ideal fit, be forthright and offer substitutes.

12. Verifying Specifics: Verify every item mentioned, such as the timetable, the cost, and any special requests or guidelines. This guarantees that no miscommunications occur.
13. Providing References: If asked, provide client feedback or references from prior customers. This may contribute to increased confidence and trust in your offerings.
14. Trial Walks: If the customer feels at ease, recommend taking the pet for a trial walk to see how they behave and determine how comfortable they are. This can be an excellent method to facilitate the shift and foster trust.
15. Contract and Payment: Ensure the client has a signed copy of the agreement and understands how payments are made. Verify that the client is aware of the invoice and the due date.
16. Follow-Up: After the consultation, send the client a follow-up email or message to express gratitude for their time and restate the main ideas covered in the discussion.

A well-conducted initial consultation is the first step in building a solid client connection and ensuring you can satisfy the customer's and their pet's demands. It creates the foundation for a fruitful collaboration and aids in building trust right away.

Contracts and Agreements

To succeed, a dog-walking business must have extensive and unambiguous contracts and agreements. These records serve to prevent misunderstandings and safeguard you and your clients. The following should be included in your agreements and contracts:

1. Contact Details: Provide the client's details, such as name, address, and phone number, along with the legal name and contact details of your dog walking service.
2. Services Offered: Specify precisely what services you will offer. Indicate the kind of walks (solo or in a group), how often they happen, and any other services (such as playing, food, or medicine administration).
3. Timetable and Scheduling: Establish the days and times for any walks or services. Make sure the program is something you and the customer agree upon.

4. Duration and Termination: Indicate if the agreement is for an indefinite period, a set term, or a predetermined number of walks. Add clauses on contract termination, such as notice requirements.
5. Pricing and Payment: Describe your services' price schedule in detail. Whether payment is made on a per-walk basis or a regular payment plan, specify how and when it is due. Any additional costs, including late payment penalties, should be made clear.
6. Cancellation Policy: Describe your cancellation policy in detail, including any applicable costs and how cancellations should be reported. Conflicts are avoided, and expectations are managed as a result.
7. Responsibility and Insurance: Indicate your responsibility limits and if you have damage, accident, or injury insurance. Ensure clients are aware of their obligations regarding the behavior and well-being of their pets.
8. Confidentiality: Include a confidentiality provision to safeguard private customer information and trade secrets.
9. Pet Health and Vaccination: Request client documentation attesting to their pets' vaccines and

medical history. This protects the dog and any other animals under your supervision.

10. Emergency Contacts: Gather and record the client's emergency contact data, including the veterinarian's information and extra contacts.
11. Key and house Access: Talk about how the client's house will be accessed and how the keys will be issued. Provide information on key exchange, security precautions, and entrance and leave procedures.
12. Agreement on Behavior: Outline your expectations for the pet's conduct on walks and any potential behavioral problems. This shows off your situation-management skills and helps you control customer expectations.
13. Dispute Resolution: Provide a provision describing the process that will be used to settle issues, such as arbitration or mediation. Doing this may keep your client relationship sound and prevent legal disputes.
14. Signature and Date: You and the customer must sign and date the contract. This attests to comprehension and agreement on both sides.

15. Review and Updates: Discuss how the contract will be reviewed and updated. You may need to change the agreement as your business and services change.
16. Legal Compliance: Verify that the terms of your agreements and contracts adhere to the national, state, and municipal laws that control pet care services. It could be wise to have legal counsel look over your paperwork.
17. Preserve Copies: Preserve hard copy and digital copies of all agreements and contracts. They function as proof of the circumstances and terms that were decided upon.

In addition to being required by law, having well-written contracts and agreements is also a good idea to guarantee clarity of expectations and safeguard your business. By carefully drafting and maintaining these documents, you may provide a solid basis to your dog-walking business.

Client Retention Strategies

Maintaining a clientele is critical to your dog-walking business's long-term prosperity and expansion. The following are some successful tactics to keep your customers coming back:

1. Exceptional Service: The most effective retention tactic is continuously offering high-quality service. Make the extra effort to guarantee the dogs' welfare and the consumers' contentment. The cornerstone of a loyal customer base is dependable, considerate, and expert service.
2. Regular Communication: Send out updates regularly to keep your consumers informed. Give them details about your visits and send them pictures and remarks about their dogs while you walk. Open and transparent communication fosters trust.
3. Personalization: Adapt your offerings to the particular requirements of each client and their pet's personality. You stand out when you demonstrate that you are aware of and concerned about their needs.
4. Loyalty Programs: Put in place incentives or loyalty programs for recurring customers. Provide special promotions, discounts, or free walks following a predetermined number of reservations. Rewards encourage customers to come back.
5. Special Occasion Recognition: Recall and honor milestones in your pet's life, such as birthdays or

adoption anniversaries. A modest card or message might be a great way to express your consideration.

6. Consistency: Maintain a continuous level of excellence and dependability in your offerings. Consistent tells customers they can count on you to give their dogs the care they require, fostering confidence.
7. Client Feedback: proactively ask for and pay attention to the recommendations and worries of your clients. Utilize their feedback to enhance your offerings and show them you respect their viewpoints.
8. Birthday Celebrations: Send a modest gift or arrange a special walk to honor the birthdays of your clients' dogs. This kind of act demonstrates your concern for their four-legged family members.
9. Special Offers & specials: Occasionally, unique specials, such as multi-walk discounts or seasonal offers. Promotions have the power to draw in new customers and boost recurring revenue.
10. Excellent Follow-Up: Send a follow-up email or message following each service to ensure your clients are happy with your attention and express gratitude for selecting your services. Prove your concern for the welfare of their pets.

11. Show Your Expertise: Keep learning about recent advancements in pet care techniques and trends. Putting your knowledge and commitment to the welfare of pets on display gives your clients trust.
12. Referral Incentives: Provide discounts or prizes to existing clients to encourage them to recommend friends and family to your services.
13. Transparent Pricing and Policies: Keep your pricing and corporate policies as transparent as possible. Customers must know your prices, cancelation procedures, and extra costs.
14. Managing Issues with Grace: When problems or worries arise, handle them tactfully and competently. Provide answers, assume accountability when necessary, and ensure the customer feels respected and heard.
15. Holiday and Vacation Services: Provide extra services to clients during their holidays or vacations. Being there for them when they need you most may make a big impression.
16. Community Involvement: Highlight your activities within the neighborhood's dog- and pet-loving community. Talk about your involvement in local

business collaborations, charitable endeavors, and events.

By implementing these client retention methods, you can improve your client relationship, win their loyalty, and lay the groundwork for your dog-walking business's long-term success. Recall that a sincere love of animals, outstanding customer service, and trust is the foundation of long-lasting client relationships.

Dealing with Difficult Clients

It might be tough to deal with demanding clients, but you can handle these circumstances well if you take the appropriate approach. Here's how to deal with challenging customers in your dog-walking business:

1. Remain Calm and Professional: When dealing with a challenging customer, maintain your composure and professionalism. Control your emotions and concentrate on finding a calm solution to the problem.
2. Active Listening: Pay close attention to the issues and grievances raised by the customer. Allow them to vent their annoyances without any interference. This demonstrates your appreciation for their input and readiness to consider other viewpoints.

3. Empathize: Exhibit understanding and empathy. Respect their emotions and annoyances, notwithstanding your disagreement with their viewpoint. Empathy eases tension and fosters communication.
4. Address the Issue: After the client has expressed their worries, deal with the matter head-on. When in doubt, seek clarity by asking questions and offering answers or justifications.
5. Provide Solutions: Make workable suggestions for resolving the current issue. This might entail changing your services, rearranging the timetable, or clearing any confusion.
6. Establish Boundaries: Be professional at all times and establish sensible limits. Communicate your boundaries and expectations clearly and courteously if the customer starts acting disrespectfully or excessively demanding.
7. Remain Positive: Keep your spirits up during the conversation. Tension can be reduced by concentrating on solutions and animal welfare.
8. Document Communication: Maintain a record of every correspondence you have with the customer. This

covers written agreements as well as emails and texts. In the event of a disagreement, documentation may be helpful.

9. Involve a Neutral Third Party: If you cannot resolve the conflict alone, you might consider bringing in an impartial third party to help you work things out, such as a mediator or a professional association.
10. Follow Your Rules: Respect the conditions of the contract and your business's rules. Reiterate your needs in a kind but firm manner if the client requests anything outside the parameters of your services or agreement.
11. Know When to Split Up: You might not always be able to please a challenging customer, even with your best efforts. It is preferable to part ways professionally and cordially in such circumstances. Not every customer is a suitable fit for your business.
12. Get Legal Counsel If Needed: If things get out of hand and you think it's essential, speak with a lawyer about your rights and responsibilities.
13. Take Care of Your Health: Challenging customers may be emotionally taxing. Take good care of your health,

ask friends or mentors for advice, and know when to leave a situation to refuel.

14. Take What You've Learned from the Experience: Every difficult customer encounter presents a chance for development. Reflect on the lessons you can take from the event and apply them to future business and client interactions.

Remember that not every customer will be a good fit, and disagreements could occasionally occur. A positive reputation for your dog walking service may be ensured by professionally, patiently, and empathetically handling problematic clients. This will assist in relieving tension and lead to mutually satisfying outcomes.

Feedback and Continuous Improvement

Receiving and analyzing feedback is crucial to maintaining and growing your dog walking business. Here's how you properly get, consider, and act upon feedback:

1. Solicit feedback: Make a conscious effort to motivate customers to offer input. Whether through online evaluations, polls, or face-to-face interactions, it is easy for people to express their opinions.

2. Stay responsive to Input: Remain open and responsive to input, regardless of its positive or bad aspects. Recall that receiving criticism is a chance for improvement.
3. Prompt Follow-Up: Ask clients what they think shortly after a service. This demonstrates your interest in their experience and allows you to resolve any issues that may arise quickly.
4. Anonymous Feedback: Give customers the choice to submit feedback anonymously if they are uncomfortable disclosing their opinions publicly. This could motivate more sincere criticism.
5. Conduct Regular Surveys: Ask clients about their opinions on many areas of your dog walking services, such as scheduling, communication, and the welfare of the pet.
6. Actively Listen: Pay attention to what the customer says and try to comprehend their point of view. Avoid becoming defensive or interjecting.
7. Thanks to customers: Thank customers for their comments and reassure them that their opinions matter and will be considered to enhance the services.

8. Classify and Examine Input: Organize input into groups to find recurring topics and problems. This study assists you in identifying areas that require enhancement.
9. Prioritize Feedback: Prioritize feedback depending on its significance and impact. Prioritize tackling urgent problems first, then more important ones.
10. Set Objectives for Improvement: Establish specific, attainable improvement targets based on the comments. Make sure these objectives are precise, quantifiable, and time bound.
11. Communication and Transparency: Keep your consumers updated on the modifications and enhancements you're doing in response to their suggestions. Building trust requires being open and honest about your resolve-to-resolve issues.
12. Training and Skill Development: Make an investment in your education and training to deal with persistent problems. Improving your abilities can shield you from future issues of this kind.
13. Track Progress: Keep tabs on your advancement in responding to criticism and accomplishing your

objectives for development. Evaluate if the modifications have been beneficial regularly.

14. Adjust to Changing Needs: Recognize that when clients' needs and expectations change, they may also. Be adaptable in how you modify your offerings to satisfy these evolving demands.
15. Honor Excellent Feedback: Give credit and recognition to customers who offer exceptional feedback or glowing references. Gaining potential clients' trust via sharing their experiences might be beneficial.
16. Share Success Stories: Make good events and comments into success tales. Present case studies or client endorsements to show how you've resolved issues and enhanced your services.
17. Continuous Feedback Loop: Create a feedback loop always open to clients' contributions. You can adjust and get better over time with regular feedback.

In addition to improving your dog walking services, customer feedback shows you are dedicated to giving pets the finest care possible. Customers value companies that proactively try to solve their issues and make their experience enjoyable.

Chapter 7: Expanding Your Dog Walking Business

(Figure: 07)

Growing your dog walking business is exciting and may bring more money and customers. Here is a calculated strategy for growth:

1. Market research: Conduct an in-depth market study before expanding to find prospects in your target location. Analyze the competitors, the need for dog walking services, and the characteristics of potential customers.
2. Geographic Expansion: If there is a need for your services in new communities or geographic locations, think about growing your business there. A few walks in the new site are an excellent place to start before progressively increasing your presence.
3. Extra Services: To reach a more significant customer, broaden the scope of your offerings. Provide pet transportation, pet sitting, or specialized care for particular breeds or needs. Offering a variety of services might help you stand out from rivals.
4. Hiring personnel: As your business expands, you might need to bring on more support personnel or dog walkers. Ensure everyone on your staff is qualified to deliver top-notch service and shares your enthusiasm for pet care.
5. Marketing and Promotion: Make marketing investments to connect with your target customers in these new markets. Use social media, local print media,

and internet advertising to advertise your extended services.

6. Website and Online Presence: Ensure your website is updated to consider your growth and the new topics you write about. To reach potential customers in your extended service regions, ensure your web presence is optimized for local search.
7. Partnerships: Work with nearby pet-related companies, such as veterinarians, pet shops, and groomers. These alliances may result in recommendations and raise your profile within the neighborhood.
8. Client Retention: Keep in mind your current clientele while you grow. Continue providing exceptional service to attract new customers and keep existing ones. To promote recurring business, think about running promotions.
9. Regulations and Licensing: Ensure you abide by all applicable laws and regulations in the new markets you are entering. There may be regional regulations about pet care services.

10. Fleet and Equipment: To accommodate a growing clientele, you might need to invest more in cars, trucks, and supplies as your business grows.
11. Scaling Systems: Implement effective scheduling and administration systems to manage higher client traffic. You may maintain high-quality service and streamline operations with software solutions.
12. Quality Control: Keep a laser-like emphasis on quality control as you grow. To guarantee customer happiness, assess your services regularly, get input from your clients, and make any required adjustments.
13. Financial Planning: Create a budget to help with the growth. Consider elements like rising overhead costs, employee pay, and marketing expenditures. Make sure your business has the resources to meet the needs of expansion.
14. Risk Management: Assess and reduce growth risks, including liability issues and insurance requirements. Speak with experts to make sure your business is sufficiently safeguarded.
15. Monitoring and Evaluation: Keep a close eye on how well your growth initiatives work. Evaluate the ROI regularly and tweak your plan, as necessary.

Planning, making a financial commitment, and staying dedicated to providing high-quality services are all necessary when growing your dog walking business. You may expand your business and satisfy the demands of a wider clientele by adhering to a well-planned strategy.

Hiring and Training Employees or Contractors

If your dog-walking business is developing, you might need more employees or contractors to meet the demand. This is a comprehensive how-to for selecting and onboarding workers or contractors:

1. Establish Your Needs: Ascertain the positions requiring filling and the duties associated with each post. This might include dog walkers, pet sitters, office workers, or even drivers for a dog walking business.
2. Write descriptions of jobs: Provide precise and comprehensive job descriptions that outline the requirements, duties, and expectations for every position. Verify with applicants that they know the responsibilities and the level of dedication needed.
3. Hiring Procedure: Post-employment positions on your website, on job boards, on social media, and in neighborhood pet-related groups, among other

platforms. To increase security and trust, do background checks on prospective hires.

4. Candidates for Interviews: Interview applicants to evaluate their qualifications, backgrounds, and personalities. Inquire about their approach to pet care, aptitude for addressing problems, and dedication to the position.
5. Verify References: Get in touch with the references that candidates have supplied to learn more about their dependability and work ethic. References from previous employment with pets might be beneficial.
6. Employee vs. Contractor: Choose between using independent contractors or hiring staff members. Contractors provide flexibility but need more training, whereas employees have greater control and carry more responsibility.
7. Training: Give staff members or contractors thorough training. This should include customer communication, corporate policies, pet first aid, and dog handling practices. Stress the value of customer pleasure and safety.
8. Onboarding Procedure: Create an onboarding procedure that acquaints new personnel with your

business's operations, values, and culture. Give them access to your scheduling and communication systems, along with any equipment that may be required.

9. Regular Meetings: Set up frequent check-ins or team meetings to keep communication lines open and handle any issues or queries. This is an additional chance to offer continuing education and updates.
10. Safety Procedures: Ensure every employee or contractor is knowledgeable about safety procedures. This covers risk management, emergency protocols, and dog behavior recommendations.
11. Remarks and Assessment: Establish a framework for performance evaluation to give helpful criticism. Regular evaluations highlight strengths and point out issues that need work.
12. Contracts and Agreements: Establish explicit contracts or agreements that specify the conditions of a contractor's engagement or employment. If necessary, include non-compete agreements, confidentiality clauses, and non-disclosure agreements.
13. Legal Compliance: If you employ people, follow all applicable employment-related rules, including

minimum wage, overtime, and payroll taxes. Consult a lawyer to make sure you are compliant.

14. Insurance and Liability: To safeguard your business in mishaps or accidents, make sure all of your contractors and workers are adequately covered by insurance.
15. Promote Professional Development: Motivate your staff to look for training courses or certifications related to pet care to advance their careers. Putting money into their expansion helps your business and the caliber of services you offer.
16. Preserve Your Business Culture: Ensure all workers and contractors share your commitment to high service standards and corporate principles.
17. Ongoing Support: Provide your staff with continuous assistance and resources, such as access to a mentor or supervisor. Deal with any issues or problems right away.

Hiring and training workers or contractors is a vital first step in growing your dog-walking business. You can preserve the level of service that distinguishes your business and guarantee the welfare of the animals in your care by carefully choosing and training your staff.

Scaling Your Operations and Services

As your dog walking business expands, scaling your operations and services is a wise strategic decision to meet rising demand. Here's an efficient way to accomplish it:

1. Assess Present Activities: Start by comprehensively assessing your present activities. Determine what needs to be improved and any possible bottlenecks that might prevent expansion.
2. Simplify Processes: Effective growth management requires you to streamline your operational procedures—Automate administrative duties like scheduling, billing, and communication to free up time for client care.
3. Invest in Technology: Use technological tools such as GPS tracking devices, client management systems, and scheduling software. These solutions help improve your business's operational effectiveness and customer service.
4. Increase the Range of Services Offered: Vary your offerings to meet the demands of a larger spectrum of customers. Consider including extra services like pet

sitting, lodging, or specialist care for particular breeds or behavioral requirements.

5. Geographic Expansion: Carefully consider your expansion strategy if you're aiming to reach new geographic regions. Analyze the new sites' demand, competitiveness, and logistical issues. Modify your offering to suit these regions' particular requirements.
6. Hiring and Training: As your business grows, you might need to bring on more support workers, dog walkers, or pet sitters. Ensure the new hires on your team are appropriately taught and in line with the standards and values of your business.
7. Fleet Management: Effectively manage your fleet if your business provides transportation services. When necessary, consider growing your fleet of vans.
8. Quality Control: Continue to give quality control priority. To guarantee customer happiness, assess your services regularly, get input from your clients, and make any required adjustments.
9. Safety and Risk Management: There is a greater chance of mishaps or events when there are more employees and clients. Put strict safety procedures

and risk management techniques into place to safeguard customers, pets, and your business.

10. Client Communication: Keep your clients informed and make booking appointments easy by sending out information regularly. Investing in CRM tools can help you efficiently manage a more extensive clientele.
11. Track Performance: Keep an eye on how well your services and operations are always doing. Examine essential performance metrics, including revenue growth, client happiness, and retention rates.
12. Customer Feedback: proactively ask for and act upon customer feedback to improve. Customer insights can guide service improvements.
13. Marketing and Promotion: Invest in marketing to advertise your broader service offerings and attract new customers. Use social media, local, and internet advertising to reach a larger audience.
14. Partnerships: To broaden your clientele and get recommendations, work with nearby pet-related companies like groomers, vets, or pet shops.
15. Financial Planning: Create a budget that aligns with your growth objective. Make a budget for higher

overhead expenses and compute your financial estimates.

16. Legal and Compliance: Ensure your business's activities abide by all applicable local, state, and federal laws. This includes any obligations for permits, insurance, and taxes that may arise from your business's expansion.
17. Pay Attention to Client Retention: Don't overlook your current clientele while you grow. Continue providing exceptional service to attract new customers and keep existing ones.
18. Create a Scalability Plan: Ensure any modifications or systems you implement are scalable. Your business should be prepared to withstand future expansion without experiencing undue disruptions.

Planning, making financial commitments, and staying dedicated to providing high-quality services are all necessary while growing your dog walking business. These procedures will help you grow your business efficiently and satisfy a wider clientele's demands while monitoring your success.

Exploring Additional Pet-Related Services

Adding other pet-related services to your dog-walking business might be wise if you want to reach a wider audience and boost sales. Take a look at these services:

1. Pet Sitting: When their owners are away, pets are looked after in their homes by pet-sitting services. In addition to house-sitting responsibilities, this might involve feeding, playing, and spending time with the pets.
2. Overnight Stays: Allowing customers to spend the night at their residences helps ease their minds on the road. This service often involves walking the pet in the morning and evening, feeding it, and providing companionship.
3. Pet Transport: Offer pet transport services to customers who might want help transporting their animals to vet visits, grooming sessions, or other locations. Make sure your car is outfitted for safe transportation and pet friendly.
4. Essential Grooming Services: Provide washing, nail cutting, ear cleaning, and brushing as essential grooming services. Between routine grooming

sessions, these services can assist in maintaining the pet's beauty and hygiene.

5. Playgroup or doggie Daycare: Set up a playgroup or doggie daycare under supervision for dogs who might benefit from group exercise and socialization. Either a full or half-day service is available.
6. Pet Training: If you are an experienced dog trainer, consider providing lessons or training sessions. This might involve socializing puppies, behavior correction, or basic obedience training.
7. Pet photography: Capturing priceless moments with pets is possible with this imaginative and enjoyable service. Pet portraits may be done in various locations, including parks or the client's house.
8. Pet Product Sales: Take into account making pet-related purchases, such as food, toys, collars, and leashes. You have two options: keep up with inventories or form alliances with vendors of pet supplies.
9. Pet Health & Wellness Services: Provide services about the health and well-being of pets, such as medication administration, nutrition monitoring, or weight-loss exercise plans.

10. Behavioral Consultations: Provide advice on problems relating to the behavior of pets. You can advise clients on better understanding their dogs' behavior and suggest methods for doing so.
11. In-house Veterinary Care: Work with vets who provide services that can be done in your house. You can become a one-stop pet care shop by enabling these services.
12. Pet First Aid and CPR Classes: Provide owners of pets with pet first aid and CPR training. Teaching them the fundamentals of emergency pet care can be a helpful service.
13. Eco-Friendly Services: Consider providing sustainable and eco-friendly pet care services like organic snacks and biodegradable trash bags.
14. Cat Sitting and Care: Adding cat care to your list of services will enable you to contact more people. Typical services include feeding and seating cats and maintaining their litter boxes.
15. House Cleaning Services: Incorporate house cleaning services with pet care. Customers who need a tidy and pet-friendly setting may find this intriguing.

Examine the demand and level of competition in your local market before branching out into new services. Ensure you and your group have the abilities and knowledge required to offer these extra services safely and competently. You may establish yourself as a more complete and competitive pet care provider in your area by providing a more comprehensive range of pet-related services.

Franchising and Partnership Opportunities

Using partnerships and franchising to develop your dog walking business might be a wise strategy to reach new areas and build your brand. Here's how to take advantage of these changes:

The Franchise:

By franchising, you enable other people to run independent branches of your dog-walking business while retaining your name, infrastructure, and customer service. This is the method to follow:

1. Business Model and Branding: Ensure your dog walking business has a recognizable, well-developed brand and a workable, replicable business plan.

2. Legal and Financial Guidance: To comprehend the laws and rules about franchising, consult an attorney. Create a concise franchise agreement that specifies the requirements for franchisees.
3. Package for Franchise: Provide a thorough franchise package including marketing materials, operating standards, training, and support. Franchisees should receive all the resources and training necessary to run their businesses profitably from this package.
4. Franchise Fees and Revenue Sharing: Establish what costs, such as upfront franchise fees, royalties, and advertising expenses, franchisees must pay to utilize your name and support. Create a transparent revenue-sharing plan that works for the franchisee and you.
5. Franchisee Selection: Create a procedure for selecting franchisees who align well with your business's beliefs and brand. This procedure could include background checks, financial evaluations, and interviews.
6. Support and Training: Give franchisees and their employees thorough training. Ensure they comprehend your business's procedures, recommended pet care practices, and customer service expectations.

7. Ongoing Support: Provide franchisees with continuous assistance. This entails constant contact, aid with advertising and promotions, and help with problems as required.
8. Quality Control: Keep a laser-like focus on quality control to ensure franchisee services meet your brand's expectations. Conduct performance reviews and evaluations regularly.
9. Expansion Strategy: Create a well-thought-out plan for using franchising to expand geographically. Choose the markets or target areas that would best support your dog-walking business.

Partnerships:

Partnerships entail working with other companies or organizations to improve your services or reach a wider audience. Here's how to look at possible partnerships:

1. Determine Possible Alliances: Seek companies or groups that enhance your dog walking offerings. Veterinarians, pet stylists, pet retailers, and pet insurance providers may fall under this category.
2. Collaborative Services: Provide packaged services by collaborating with partners. For instance, you may

collaborate with a vet to offer wellness check-ups as part of pet care packages.

3. Cross-Promotion: To reach each other's clientele, work together on marketing projects like cross-promotional campaigns. This might involve exchanging marketing materials or providing group discounts.
4. Referral Programs: Establish programs wherein you and your partners direct clients to each other's services. Client confidence may be built this way, benefiting both sides.
5. Networking and Events: Participate in local networking events and pet-related activities. These gatherings offer chances to meet possible partners.
6. Online Presence: Use your website and social media accounts to highlight your collaborations. Emphasize the advantages for clients and their pets of these partnerships.
7. Legal Agreements: To specify the conditions and obligations of the partnership, draft explicit legal agreements with your partners. Seek legal advice to guarantee the protection of all parties.

Building your dog walking business through partnerships or franchising can provide growth prospects and allow you to use other people's or businesses' skills. It's critical to approach these possibilities with due diligence, adherence to the law, and a dedication to upholding the caliber and standing of your brand.

Managing Finances and Tax Considerations

Effective financial management and tax compliance are essential for your dog-walking business's legality and profitability. Key actions to guarantee both tax compliance and financial stability are as follows:

1. Keep Your Personal and Business Finances Apart: Keep distinct financial records and bank accounts for your personal and business spending. Tax compliance and financial transparency depend on this division.
2. Accounting System: To monitor revenue, spending, and general financial health, implement an accounting system or employ accounting software. To keep organized, update your books regularly.
3. Making a budget: Make a budget that lists all of your anticipated costs and revenue. A budget aids financial

planning for the future and enables you to make well-informed business decisions.

4. Tax Identification Number (TIN): If you have workers, apply for an Employer Identification Number (EIN) or Tax Identification Number (TIN). In addition to being used for taxes, this number could be needed for bank and legal activities.
5. Money Tracking: Maintain a close eye on all earnings, including tips, payments from clients, and any additional sources of money derived from providing dog walking services.
6. Expense Tracking: Keep a careful eye on all your business spending, including supplies for pet care, auto repairs, insurance, advertising, and training. Maintaining accurate records may result in tax deductions.
7. Tax Deductions: Recognize the tax breaks for your dog walking business. Deductions for home office space, car expenditures, professional development, and other expenses may fall under this category.
8. Quarterly Estimated Taxes: You could pay the IRS quarterly estimated taxes if your business brings in a

sizable amount of money. To find out what taxes you owe, speak with a tax expert.

9. Insurance: Make sure your business has enough coverage. Purchasing professional liability insurance can shield you from potential financial obligations in mishaps or accidents.
10. Emergency Fund: Establish an emergency fund to deal with unforeseen costs or business interruptions. Financial security requires having a cushion of money.
11. Pricing Structure: Make sure your prices account for all costs of running your firm, including your income. Ensure you're charging a fair price for your services without sacrificing profitability.
12. Invoices and Receipts: Prepare expert invoices for your services and maintain duplicates of all invoices and receipts about out-of-pocket costs. These records are necessary for both tax and record-keeping purposes.
13. Retirement Planning and Savings: Consider using individual retirement accounts (IRAs) or other retirement plans to save money for your future. Making financial plans for the future is crucial.

14. Tax Compliance: Keep up with the relevant tax laws for your business. Make sure you comply with all applicable local, state, and federal tax regulations by speaking with an accountant or tax specialist.
15. Financial Planning: Examine your finances regularly and make plans. This might entail managing debt, establishing financial objectives, and making wise choices regarding the expansion of your business.
16. Consult with Experts: To ensure you optimize tax advantages and handle your finances skillfully, get guidance from financial experts, such as accountants or tax counselors.

Effective management of finances and tax planning are critical components of operating a profitable dog-walking business. Financial stability and legal compliance can result from careful planning and following best practices in finance.

Chapter 8: Challenges, Pitfalls, and Long-Term Success

(Figure: 08)

Running a dog walking business inevitably involves obstacles and mistakes, but resolving these problems may create the conditions for long-term success. A discussion of these components follows:

Problems:

Managing a dog walking business might include several difficulties. The main problem is the competition. Setting your business apart is crucial in the fiercely competitive pet care sector. The unpredictable nature of the work presents another difficulty. Weather, last-minute cancellations, and dog behavior may throw off your routine. It might be challenging to balance meeting customer expectations while ensuring dogs are always safe and well.

Furthermore, finding and keeping competent employees might be difficult. Finding dependable, committed staff members as passionate about pet care as you are crucial. Last but not least, if the job's physical demands—such as walking or managing several dogs—are not adequately addressed, they may result in weariness or injury.

Difficulties: Dog walking companies need to know a few typical challenges. Competing by underpricing services might put a burden on your finances and diminish the value of your experience. Ignoring adequate insurance and legal safeguards puts your business in danger of liability. Financial difficulties and tax complications can result from improper financial management and inadequate record-keeping. Your business's reputation and client connections may suffer from subpar customer service or communication.

Another mistake is to undervalue the significance of continuing education and professional development. If your knowledge and abilities become stagnant, you may find adjusting to changing pet care procedures and industry standards more difficult. Instability and financial strain can also result from overexpansion without enough planning or financial resources.

Prolonged Achievement:

You must overcome these obstacles and avoid traps to succeed in the dog walking business long-term. Establishing a solid reputation and brand is crucial. Prioritize delivering excellent services, having clear communication, and having a love for caring for pets. Make ongoing investments in your professional development to keep abreast of market developments and best practices.

You may reach a wider audience and keep clients by maintaining a strong online and offline presence, including a business website and active social media participation. You may cultivate a devoted clientele by providing exceptional customer service and client relationship management.

Long-term financial stability and development depend heavily on strategic financial planning, which includes maintaining accurate records, establishing competitive yet profitable prices, and paying taxes as required. If you want to grow your firm without sacrificing quality, consider partnering with other companies or expanding your service offerings.

Long-term success in the dog walking industry ultimately boils to commitment, flexibility, and a sincere love for animals. Your business may prosper and expand through proactive problem-solving, avoiding typical traps, and unwavering dedication to your customers and their dogs.

Overcoming Common Challenges in the Dog Walking Business

While owning a dog walking business has its advantages, it also presents a unique set of difficulties. These issues must be resolved for your business to expand and be sustainable over the long run. Here is a thorough explanation of typical problems in the dog-walking business, along with solutions:

1. Competition and Market Saturation: Difficulty: The dog walking market is not an exception to the pet care industry's reputation for fierce competition. It might be challenging to stand out in the market when so many dog-walking services are available.
   Strategy: Emphasize specialization and distinctiveness to get beyond this obstacle. Consider providing distinctive services like puppy training, pet sitting, or care tailored to particular breeds. Gaining a specialized clientele might help you stand out from the competition. Make strategic branding and marketing investments to emphasize your service's distinctive qualities.
2. Uncertain Work Environments: Challenge: The weather and last-minute cancellations can make a dog walker's everyday job uneasy because dogs behave differently.
   Strategy: It's crucial to have a solid system and be flexible. Create backup plans for anything unforeseen, such as hostile conduct or lousy weather. Use scheduling software to keep organized and have open contact lines with your clients. The secret to handling

these uncertainties is to be adaptable and ready to change your plans as circumstances demand.

3. Hiring and Retaining Qualified Staff: Difficulty: Finding and keeping trustworthy workers with the necessary skills might be difficult. Dog walkers should have the required training and have a strong love for caring for pets.

   Strategy: Use a rigorous screening procedure when recruiting to get beyond this obstacle. Verify references, run background checks, and ensure the prospects have the same values as your business. Provide extensive training courses so your employees have the required knowledge and abilities. To improve employee retention, provide a good work environment that offers competitive pay and room for advancement within the organization.

4. Physical Demands and Safety Concerns: Difficulty: The job's physical demands, such as walking or managing several dogs, can cause weariness and raise safety issues for the dogs and the dog walker.

   Strategy: Ensure everyone on your staff knows safe dog handling procedures. Assign proper gear, such as harnesses, leashes, and first aid kits. Encourage yourself and your team to exercise regularly and self-care to avoid burnout and injuries. Stress the need for safety precautions, particularly under erratic circumstances.

5. Client Expectations and Contact: Difficulty: Because clients may have varying opinions about the range of services or preferred methods of communication, it can be challenging to set and manage client expectations.
   Strategy: To tackle this issue, immediately establish explicit guidelines and standards. In your contracts, include your services, prices, and cancellation procedures. Keep the lines of communication open by providing frequent updates, holding feedback sessions, and quickly answering questions. Use technology to your advantage by streamlining client interactions and giving them real-time information about their pets, such as scheduling applications or communication platforms.
6. Operational Efficiency: Difficulty: Managing a dog walking business's daily operation effectively can be difficult. Invoicing, managing records, and scheduling may be labor-intensive and error prone.

Strategy: To improve efficiency, spend money on technological solutions like client management programs or scheduling software. By automating scheduling, billing, and client communications, these solutions free up your time so you can concentrate on giving dogs the best care possible. Create effective record-keeping procedures to guarantee that you correctly monitor customer information and retain well-organized financial records.

7. Legal and Liability worries: Difficulty: Dog walking firms may face many legal difficulties and liability concerns related to pet accidents or property damage. Strategy: Invest in complete insurance protection for your business, including professional liability and liability insurance. Speak with legal experts to comprehend and handle legal issues like contracts and client agreements. Robust safety procedures and risk management techniques should be implemented to reduce the possibility of mishaps.
8. Client Retention and Growth: Challenge: Maintaining a clientele is essential to your business's long-term viability. Furthermore, expanding your clientele and

drawing in new business might be difficult in a cutthroat industry.

Strategy: Focus on developing enduring client connections by going above and beyond for your customers. Provide loyalty programs or referral bonuses to promote word-of-mouth recommendations and repeat business. To increase your reach, spend money on marketing initiatives like social media marketing, internet advertising, and joint ventures with nearby pet-related companies. Ensure your growth tactics are permanently evaluated considering current market trends and customer demands.

9. Financial Management: Challenge: Pricing, budgeting, and tax compliance are all critical components of successful financial management for your dog walking business.

   Strategy: To correctly manage your funds, create a solid budget. Establish pricing systems that ensure you stay profitable while being competitive and pay all of your business's expenditures, including your compensation.

10. Burnout and Self-Care: Challenge: Maintain accurate records of your income and spending. You may also want to consult with accountants or financial advisors to manage your money and ensure you comply with tax laws. Employees and business owners alike may experience stress and burnout due to the demands of the dog-walking industry.

    Strategy: Give self-care and work-life harmony top priority. Ensure your staff has opportunities for rest and encourage them to take regular breaks. As the business's owner, you should lead by example by efficiently handling your workload and assigning work, as necessary. Establish unambiguous guidelines for working hours and rest periods to avoid burnout.

To overcome these typical obstacles in the dog walking industry, one must combine forethought, flexibility, and a dedication to providing high-quality service. You may overcome these challenges and lay the groundwork for sustained success in the field by putting these techniques into practice.

Staying Informed About Industry Trends

Maintaining a competitive advantage, accommodating shifting customer preferences, and safeguarding the welfare of the pets under your care depends on keeping up to date on industry trends in the ever-evolving dog-walking profession. Here are some tips to keep you abreast of the most recent developments in the industry:

1. Websites and Industry Publications: Regularly read trade journals, periodicals, and dog walking and pet care websites. These resources frequently include news, articles, and analyses on cutting-edge techniques, new technology, and developing trends.
2. Expert Organizations: Be a member of organizations and professional groups for pet care, such as Pet Sitters International (PSI) or the National Association of Professional Pet Sitters (NAPPS). These organizations provide information on industry advances through their resources, bulletins, and networking opportunities.
3. Attend trade exhibits, conferences, and seminars tailored to your sector. These gatherings allow people

to network and discover the newest innovations, best practices, and trends in dog walking and pet care.

4. Participate in social media groups, internet forums, and communities devoted to dog walking and pet care. You may stay informed and acquire insights into industry trends by participating in conversations and exchanging experiences with colleagues.
5. Market Research: Do some market research to determine your target audience's wants and needs. Frequent surveys or client feedback can yield important insights into changing trends and client expectations.
6. Blogs and Vlogs: Keep up with industry-related blogs and vlogs produced by experts in the sector. Many knowledgeable dog walkers and pet care specialists share their knowledge, trends, and observations through these networks.
7. Continuing Education: Spend money on training courses, canine behavior, and pet care seminars. Continued education can help you stay current when new methods and information are developed as the industry changes.

8. Updates on Technology and Software: Remain up to speed on developments in software and technology that affect your business. Use scheduling and management software with the newest integrated features to optimize your operations.
9. Collaborations and Networking: Form alliances and expand your network with nearby pet-related businesses, like groomers, trainers, pet shops, and doctors. Working together with these experts can lead to prospects for referrals and reveal new trends.
10. Client Input: Seek input from your clients on their changing requirements and expectations by promoting candid communication. Utilize this knowledge to modify your procedures and offerings.
11. Track Rivals: Keep a watch on what your rivals are up to. Examine their offerings regarding services, costs, and customer interaction tactics to find emerging market trends.
12. Examine industry surveys and studies since they frequently offer information and analysis on market changes and industry trends. These studies can provide insightful information on how the sector is developing.

13. Regulatory Changes: Keep yourself updated on any alterations or revisions to local regulations about dog walking and pet care. It is essential to abide by municipal, state, and federal laws.

You may position your dog-walking business to adapt and grow in a continually changing sector by actively searching out information from numerous sources and continuing your education. By keeping up with current developments in the field, you can maintain your edge, provide cutting-edge solutions, and adapt to the evolving requirements of your customers and their cherished pets.

Adapting to Changing Circumstances and Regulations

Flexibility is essential in the dog walking industry, mainly when dealing with shifting conditions and changing laws. Here are some tips for successfully adapting so that your business may continue to be profitable and compliant:

1. Remain Informed: Keep track of all applicable local, state, and federal rules regularly. This covers leash restrictions, regulations regarding animal care, licensing requirements, and any law changes that can impact your business. Subscribe to trade periodicals,

news updates, and pertinent government websites to keep updated.

2. Attorney at Law: Consult legal counsel when rules change to learn how they may affect your business. You can get assistance navigating legal difficulties and contact counsel on compliance from an attorney focusing on small companies or pet-related services.
3. Modify Operations: Be ready to modify your operations if new restrictions impact how you can run your dog walking service. For example, if leash rules are strengthened, put in place training programs to guarantee that dogs behave correctly when wearing a leash. Ensure you and your employees get the required permissions if new or altered licensing requirements are made.
4. Insurance Updates: Make sure your plans are up to date with the latest rules by reviewing them. If necessary, modify your coverage to comply with new specifications. Getting comprehensive liability insurance to safeguard your business from any legal troubles is essential.
5. Client Communication: Inform your clients of any modifications to the law that could affect your

services or their pets. Open communication and transparency may support maintaining trust and managing expectations.

6. Training and Education: Invest in continuous training and education for yourself and your employees to guarantee compliance with new rules. This might entail taking classes on safety procedures, legal requirements, and pet care.
7. Operational Flexibility: Make your business plan adaptable. Be ready to adjust to situations that change due to unexpected occurrences, new rules, or changes in client needs. A flexible business structure can better handle difficulties.
8. Digital Solutions: Use technology to change course as needed. To make regulatory compliance more accessible, use scheduling software and management solutions to rapidly adjust appointments, interact with clients, and keep correct records.
9. Safety Protocols: Update your safety protocols often to stay current with new laws and industry best practices. Ensure that your staff regularly follows these practices and has received proper training.

10. Public Relations: Communicate your compliance and pet safety dedication to preserve a favorable public image. Demonstrate to your customers and the neighborhood that you run a trustworthy and considerate dog-walking service.
11. Community Involvement: Get involved with your area's authorities and community. Build strong ties with pertinent institutions, including local government offices or animal control. Being an engaged and accountable community member may benefit you.
12. Client Contracts: Examine and amend your client contracts to consider any new laws or modifications to your services. To guarantee mutual understanding and compliance, clearly define your duties and those of the client.

Adapting to shifting conditions and laws is an ongoing effort in the dog walking industry. Through knowledge-based learning, expert advice, and a proactive approach to compliance, you can successfully manage regulatory shifts and guarantee your business's legal stability and prosperity.

Planning for the Long-Term Success of Your Business

Extensive success in the dog walking industry necessitates meticulous preparation, flexibility, and a dedication to offering top-notch pet care. These actions will assist you in making plans:

1. Set Specific Objectives: Identify your long-term business objectives. These may include bringing in more clients, introducing fresh services, or boosting sales. Having specific goals gives your business direction.
2. Business Plan: Create a thorough business plan that details your objectives, strategies, goals, and vision. Provide a complete operational approach, marketing strategies, and financial estimates. Update your plan often to account for shifts in the market and your business.
3. Financial Management: Establish a financial strategy that includes investing, savings, and budgeting techniques. Keep an eye on your money, control your spending, and ensure you save for retirement and unforeseen events.

4. Service Diversification: To reach a more comprehensive customer, consider expanding your range of services. Increasing your income streams may be accomplished by branching into allied services like pet sitting, training, or grooming.
5. Client Retention: Put your energy into creating enduring bonds with your clients. To promote recurring business, deliver excellent service, communicate clearly, and offer loyalty programs.
6. Marketing Strategy: Make constant adjustments to your plan to stay current with emerging trends. To increase your reach, stay involved on social media, spend money on internet advertising, and investigate joint ventures with nearby pet-related companies.
7. Training and Education: Invest in your staff and your ongoing education. Keep abreast of evolving best practices and industry trends. Adjust to new methods and technology in the pet care industry.
8. Legal and Insurance Compliance: Check your insurance and legal compliance regularly. Ensure your current agreements and contracts.
9. Operational Efficiency: Put in place adequate mechanisms for operations. Use software and

technology to expedite communication, scheduling, and record-keeping.

10. Keeping an Eye on Rivals: Pay attention to the tactics used by your rivals. Examine what is effective for them and find areas where your business might improve.
11. Community Engagement: Make a good impression on the people in your neighborhood. Take part in events, provide instructional seminars, and interact with neighborhood pet organizations to position your business as a reliable and reputable source for pet care.
12. Adaptability: Make being flexible a fundamental skill. Accept change and be prepared to modify your plans and offerings in response to changing customer demands and market circumstances.
13. Succession Planning: If you own a business, consider creating a succession plan. This entails figuring out an exit plan or successor. Long-term planning should take into account your business's prospects after you leave.
14. Work-Life Balance: Make work-life balance a top priority to avoid burnout and keep your business

enthusiastic. Assign responsibilities, take pauses, and set aside time for rest and personal development.

15. Feedback and Improvement: Ask for customer and staff input to improve your services. Evaluate your business model regularly and look for ways to improve it.
16. Environmental Responsibilities: Consider implementing eco-friendly procedures in your business. Sustainable business methods, trash reduction initiatives, and environmentally friendly pet care items are a few examples.

Being proactive in responding to shifting conditions and consumer preferences is essential for dog-walking businesses to succeed over the long run. You may set up your business for long-term success and development by being knowledgeable, making thoughtful plans, and offering first-rate pet care.

Celebrating Milestones and Achievements

Acknowledging and celebrating successes in your dog walking business is a fulfilling experience for you and your staff and an excellent opportunity to express thanks to your customers and serve as a valuable source of inspiration. Here are some suggestions for honoring these occasions:

1. Client Appreciation Events: Plan activities that show your appreciation for your clients, such as dog-friendly playdates, picnics, or informative seminars on pet care. This improves client connections while also demonstrating your gratitude for them.
2. Appreciation of Workers: Acknowledge your staff members' efforts and commitment. Think of presenting monthly or annual prizes to the finest dog walker, the most improved employee, or the customer service champion—reward milestone achievement with bonuses, promotions, or other incentives.
3. Pet-Themed Parties: Throw pet-themed gatherings to commemorate milestones like your business's anniversary or a particular clientele size. Provide pet-friendly activities, pet contests, and freebies for customers and their animal companions.
4. Charity Events: Honor significant anniversaries by contributing to the community. Plan charitable activities that benefit animal welfare groups, such as dog walks or fundraisers. This shows your dedication

to pet care in addition to honoring your accomplishments.

5. Social Media Highlights: Post your victories and significant anniversaries on social media. Share pictures, success stories, and heartfelt notes to interact with and encourage your online community.
6. Customer References: Put customer endorsements and success stories on your website and marketing collateral. This gives social verification of your high-quality services and showcases your accomplishments.
7. Freebies and Contests: Use email newsletters or social media to host freebies or contests for your clientele. Give out rewards or discounts for participating, like a free service for the 100th customer to schedule a walk.
8. Special Discounts: To commemorate anniversaries or to attain a particular clientele, provide one-time discounts. This might encourage new business and express gratitude to your network of devoted patrons.
9. Thank-You letters: Give your clients and staff individual thank-you cards or letters. Make them feel

valued and appreciated by expressing your appreciation for their support and allegiance.

10. Press Releases and Media Coverage: Send press releases to inform the local media about your accomplishments. Appearing in regional media may establish a reputation and draw in new business.
11. Team Building Exercises: Plan team-building exercises to honor accomplishments among your employees. This encourages community, mutual action, and a healthy work atmosphere.
12. Certificate of Appreciation: Make certificates expressing gratitude to your staff and customers. It might act as a tangible memento of your appreciation for their support of your business.
13. Business Milestone Plaques: Consider making milestone plaques to showcase your business's years of existence, clientele, and other noteworthy accomplishments. These plaques may be put on display at your business's site.
14. Client Loyalty Programs: Create client loyalty programs that provide special privileges, savings, or extras to customers who have been with you for a

predetermined time or have recommended new customers to your business.

15. Take Stock of Your Journey and Set New Objectives: Make the most of landmarks to take stock of your journey and plan for the future. Honoring prior successes might inspire you to take on new challenges.

Acknowledging and applauding successes and milestones is a great way to show appreciation and improve your rapport with customers and staff. It helps preserve your dog-walking business's favorable reputation and may catalyze further expansion and prosperity.

Conclusion

After taking this tour of the dog-walking industry, we hope you better understand what it takes to launch and operate a profitable dog-walking business. This book has given you the information and resources to start this rewarding project, regardless of whether you love dogs, the great outdoors, or entrepreneurship.

Creating a successful business that meets the needs of dogs and their owners is more important than simply selling leashes and wagging tails when starting a dog walking business. You now know how important it is to comprehend the pet business, the demand for dog walking services, and the advantages of working in this field. You've learned about the knowledge and expertise required to guarantee the security and welfare of the dogs in your care and the significance of good customer service and communication.

The practical aspects of dog walking have been covered in this book, including equipment, cost, service options, and scheduling. We have discussed how critical marketing, branding, and cultivating enduring customer connections are to your business's success. Additionally, you've been prepared to deal with potential difficulties and dangers in the dog walking sector and adjust to evolving rules and conditions.

You are prepared to start your dog-walking adventure since you have acquired knowledge, enthusiasm, and a profound respect for your four-legged friends. Recall that it will need commitment to ongoing progress, hard work, and devotion, just like any other business. The valuable benefits of this line of work are the gratification of knowing you're improving the lives of dogs, the happiness of your clients, and the sheer delight of spending your days outside.

We'll encourage you to set lofty goals and have big dreams. Your enthusiasm and commitment will be your most significant advantages, regardless of whether your objective is to launch a little neighborhood dog walking service or to grow your business and take advantage of new prospects in the pet sector. We hope your dog walking business succeeds and you have lots of happy barks, wagging tails, and the best dog companionship.

Printed in Great Britain
by Amazon

37774341R00106